THE STORY OF
BIRDS
OF
NORTH AMERICA

Reviewed for Scientific Accuracy

by Lisa McGraw, Former Secretary

The Linnaean Society of New York

PICTURES by ANNE LEWIS

THE STORY OF
BIRDS
of
NORTH AMERICA

by RUTH LELLAH WHEELER

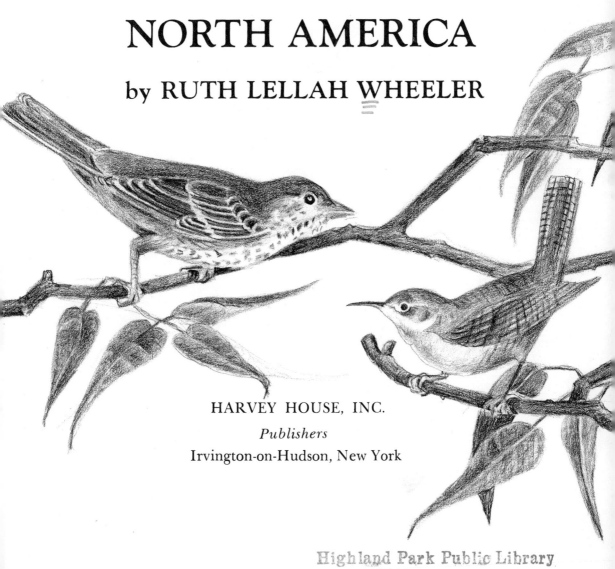

HARVEY HOUSE, INC.

Publishers

Irvington-on-Hudson, New York

A Story of Science Series Book

HARVEY HOUSE, INC. · *Publishers*

Irvington-on-Hudson, New York

© 1965 by Harvey House, Inc.

Library of Congress Catalog Card No.: 65-14630
Manufactured in the United States of America

Contents

1 Red-headed Woodpecker

2 Catbird

3 Purple Gallinule

4 Killdeer

5 Eastern Bluebird

6 Cardinal

7 Hooded Warbler

8 Robin

I

The New Land

It was early spring more than a hundred years ago. A party of pioneers hitched their teams to their wagons and formed a line on the prairie. They were driving west to find new homes. The guide raised his hand and shouted, "Stretch out!" The drivers cracked their whips and started their teams of mules

Trumpeter Swans
(About 66")

Canada Goose
(32-40")

or their yokes of oxen. The wagon train rolled on and the covered wagons creaked over the rough road along the river.

Flocks of water birds flew up from the swamps and turned toward the north. A long V of great, white birds crossed the sky. The travelers stopped to watch the strong wing-beats of the Trumpeter Swans. They heard the birds bugling in a wild chorus. Other Swans on the river beat their way up into the air, circled, and formed a V, following the leader northward. Soon their hoarse calls were lost in the distance.

Thousands of smaller water birds followed the Swans. All day the lines wavered across the sky. As the pioneers camped for the evening, they saw flocks of birds coming in from the south and settling on the river. The rushing of their wings and the music of their calls filled the air.

High above, in the full light of the setting sun, a flock of birds—pure white except for their black wing tips—passed over. They turned and came down on the prairie. The birds stood nearly as tall as a man. They stretched their long necks and looked about them. Their strong bills were as sharp as daggers, and their foreheads were red.

The clamor of their cries seemed deafening. These were the Whooping Cranes, the loudest voices on the prairie. The big Cranes stalked out on the plains and began hunting for prairie dogs, frogs, lizards, and other small game.

Darkness came. The pioneers put out their campfires and went to bed in their wagons. But all night long they heard the deep, throaty whooping of the Cranes, and the trumpeting of the Swans mingled with the calls of the smaller birds.

Snow Geese
(23-28")

When the pioneers at last drove into the valley of California, it was autumn. Birds were coming back from their northern nesting grounds. Myriads of Snow Geese, like giant snowflakes, swirled over the marshes. Again came the deep calls of the Trumpeter Swans. Thousands of the great birds were settling down on the swamps to spend the winter.

Condors

The pioneers saw a bird even larger than the Swans and the Cranes. The Condor is a great, black Vulture, almost extinct. It glides over the valleys on wings that are about ten feet from tip to tip. The Condor seldom flaps its wings. Instead, it glides and soars. Sometimes it circles above the hills on the rising currents of air for an hour or more without beating its great wings.

California Condor
(About 50")

More and more pioneers followed the first wagon trains. Some of these people settled on the prairies. They plowed up the buffalo grass and planted wheat and corn. They built fences to make pastures for their cattle. They shot the Ducks and killed the Trumpeter Swans and the Whooping Cranes.

In the West, the settlers drained the swamps where birds had stayed all winter. They plowed the fields and planted orchards. Gradually, the birds were crowded out.

The pioneers who crossed the plains saw great herds of buffalo, elk, antelope, and grizzly bears, as well as the flocks of huge birds. Now there is no buffalo left on the prairies. A few herds live in parks, but the wild ones are gone. The elk and the antelope have been driven to secluded places in the hills, and the last grizzly in the valley has long since been killed.

The Whooping Cranes are nearly gone, and the Trumpeter Swans live in protected areas. The Condor is found only in wild areas of brushy hills. Game wardens watch over these birds, and no one may hike through Condor country without a special permit.

A pair of Condors raise only one chick every other year. Many things can happen to this youngster. In a few years perhaps there will not be any Condors left to soar over the hills on motionless wings.

Passenger Pigeons

A hundred years ago no one dreamed that the most common bird in America at that time would some day be extinct. In those days countless numbers of Passenger Pigeons fed on the acorns and beechnuts in the forests of central and eastern United States.

12

Passenger Pigeons
(About 16")

The bird artist, John James Audubon, told of flocks of Pigeons that covered the sky as far as he could see in every direction. All day the living torrent moved overhead. "The light of the noonday was obscured as by an eclipse of the sun," Audubon wrote. For three days the flood of birds continued.

Audubon rode to the place where the birds roosted at night. The Pigeons came in soon after sundown. The noise of their wings stirring up strong currents of air sounded like a hurricane. So many birds lighted on the limbs of the trees that sometimes the limbs broke, and branches and birds fell together. The birds kept up a continual clamor all night. From a distance it sounded like hundreds of little bells ringing at the same time.

Whooping Cranes
(About 50")

14

The great flocks of Passenger Pigeons were one of the wonders of the world. In Wisconsin, there was a nesting site nearly seventy-five miles long and ten miles wide. Every tree in the region held at least five to ten nests, some of the larger trees holding fifty or more. It was estimated that there were one hundred thirty-six million birds in that one flock. In winter, according to early reports, the settlers in Virginia found Pigeons in flocks beyond number.

What happened to the flocks of Pigeons? They are gone. No child has ever seen a Passenger Pigeon, and no one ever will.

The settlers who came into the country wanted to farm. They cut down the thick forests which the Pigeons needed for nesting places and for food. Hunters shot the birds to use as food for themselves and to sell in the markets.

Sometimes sportsmen came out from the cities and shot birds just for fun. Many people felt that this did no harm, for there were billions of Pigeons. But in a few years there were millions instead of billions, and twenty or more years later there were thousands. After the country was settled, there were only scattered flocks of two or three hundred birds.

Finally, there were no flocks at all. On September 1, 1914, the very last Passenger Pigeon, so far as we know, died in the Cincinnati Zoological Gardens, Ohio.

It is too late to save the Passenger Pigeons, and perhaps it is too late to save the Whooping Crane and the Condor, but the people of the United States can save some other birds that have become scarce. It should be the concern of everyone in the United States to help protect our wildlife.

Cardinal
(About 9½″)

2

Structure of a Bird

Many people think that birds are the most interesting animals in the world. It surely is true that they are the brightest colored and that they make the pleasantest sounds of all animals. But whether they are red, like a Cardinal; or brown, like a Wren; or whether they sing, like a Thrush; or croak, like a Crow; birds are fascinating friends.

If I should ask you, "What is a bird?" you would probably answer without even taking time to think, "It is an animal that flies." Your answer would be partly right and partly wrong. Animals, such as bats, fly, but not all birds fly.

Hermit Thrush
(6-7")

"It's an animal that lays eggs," you try again. But that is not entirely correct, for there are mammals that lay eggs, and snakes that lay eggs. (A mammal is an animal that feeds its young with its own milk.)

"It's an animal with feathers," you keep on guessing. This time you are right. Birds have feathers, and animals that have feathers are birds. Feathers identify birds just as hair and fur identify mammals.

Birds' feathers are strong and light. Some scientists claim that, for their weight, feathers are stronger than steel. Even a bird's bones are different from those of other animals. Birds' bones are thin and hollow and are braced inside like the wings of a sailplane. Perhaps it would be better to say that the wings of a sailplane are patterned after those of a bird. The bracing in both makes them strong.

Since birds have air sacs in their bodies, they are comparatively light in weight. The air sacs are connected with the lungs, and they also open into the hollow bones. The air sacs not only decrease the weight of the bird, but they also serve to cool its fast-acting muscles. More than half the air a bird breathes may be used for cooling purposes.

A bird's shape helps it glide smoothly through the air, its bill leading. There is nothing to break the smooth contour. The wings end in a thin trailing edge. The flight feathers bend and turn, thus helping to lift. The tail, which is thin and smooth, moves like a rudder guiding the bird in flight and is used as a brake when the bird makes a landing.

In order to lessen wind resistance, birds "retract their landing gears" as most fast airplanes do. During flight, they hold their feet against their bodies. Some small birds tuck their legs close into their feathers. Birds with long legs let their feet trail out behind them.

Fish Crow
(About 17")

Living Airplanes

Birds are like living airplanes. They can fly hundreds of miles on the energy they store up in their small bodies.

A bird is a warm-blooded animal with a high body temperature. Human beings have a body temperature of 98.6° when they are well. But a bird can be healthy with a temperature ten to twelve degrees higher. A small bird, such as the Ruby-throated Hummingbird, can dash about the garden with a temperature that would send you to the hospital. A bird breathes rapidly and its heart beats rapidly. If you hold a small bird in your hand, you will feel its heart beating faster than you can count.

Ruby-throated Hummingbird
(3-3¼")

Species, Families, and Orders

Scientists have distributed birds into species, families, and orders. A *species* is a particular kind of bird, such as a Robin, a Song Sparrow, or a Brown Creeper. A *family* is a group of species which are alike in body structure and in many of their habits. The Robin, the Thrasher, and the Wood Thrush are species that are grouped into the Thrush family.

Brown Thrasher
(10-12″)

Robin
(About 10″)

Wood Thrush
(7½-8½″)

Bird families are grouped into *orders*. The Thrush family, the Sparrow family, the Lark family, and many others, form the largest of all orders—the order of perching birds. Scientists classify a bird in this way: *species,* Robin; *family,* Thrush; *order,* Perching Birds.

Meadowlark
(About 9")

Blackbird
(About 9")

The color of a bird helps to identify the species, since each species has a definite color pattern. The Meadowlark, a bird of the open fields, is identified by its yellow breast with a black necklace around it. But a bird family can not be identified by color alone. The Meadowlark and the Blackbird are members of the same family though their colors are different. Scientists place them in the same family because of the similarity in their bills and in their bodies.

21

Red-headed Woodpecker
(8½-9½")

About Bills, Feet, and Wings

One of the important clues that help to identify a family is the bird's bill. Its bill tells what kind of food the bird eats and where it finds its food. Woodpeckers are forest birds. Their food is mostly insects, which are found under the bark of trees. These birds have strong, sharp bills adapted for digging and prying for food. They have long slim tongues with sharp points, barbs, on the end. The Woodpecker digs a hole in the bark of a tree, runs its tongue into the hole, spears the insect, and drags it out.

Another clue in identifying a bird is its feet. These differ according to where the bird lives. Ducks, since they spend most of their time on the water, have big, webbed feet. Swallows are small, swift-flying birds that scoop their food out of the air with their mouths. These birds have weak feet that scarcely hold them up. By the shape of the feet you can also tell whether the bird catches its food in its claws or whether it scratches for seeds under the shrubs.

Wanderer Albatross
(About 48")

Birds' wings help us to find out how each bird lives. Some birds spend most of their lives in the air. One large bird, the Albatross, can follow a ship at sea for days. It soars and glides along on the air currents without using much muscle power. Its long, slender wings may be ten feet or more across. Other birds, such as Quail, which live in the grassy meadows, have short, broad wings and can fly only a few hundred feet at a time.

Size is also a help in identifying birds. Well-known birds are used as a scale. Birds are Warbler size, four to five inches; Sparrow size, five to six and one-half inches; Robin size, eight to ten inches; Pigeon size, thirteen to sixteen inches; Crow size,

Nuthatches
(5-6¾")

seventeen to twenty-one inches. If you become acquainted with these familiar birds, you will be able to identify a new bird by comparing its size with that of a bird you already know.

Bird Habits and Flight Patterns

As you watch the birds, you begin to realize that each species has some small identifying habit that helps you to recognize it. If a small bird runs up a tree, turns around, and runs down again, clinging to the bark, you can be quite sure it is some kind of Nuthatch. If it goes up a tree in spiral fashion and then flies down to the base of another and starts up again, it must be a Brown Creeper.

The way a bird flies helps you to identify it. Each species has its own pattern of flight. Woodpeckers have a bounding

Barn Swallows
(5½-7½″)

flight. They fly with quick wing beats, then folding their wings tightly against their bodies, they shoot forward like an arrow. They repeat this flight pattern over and over and seem to be bounding through the air as they fly across a valley.

Some small birds, such as Sparrows, fly in a jerky way. Their tails jerk up and down as the birds flutter through the air. Other birds, such as the Swallows, fly swiftly, dashing about and changing direction suddenly. A Crow flies in a straight line, with slow, steady wing beats. On the other hand, a Hummingbird moves its wings so fast that they are just a blur as it flits from flower to flower. This little "helicopter" can suspend itself in the air near a flower and then back away.

In addition to the Albatross, there are other soaring birds that use the lift of the air to carry them. Hawks and Vultures spread their wide wings and glide until they come to a thermal. A thermal is a rising bubble of light, warm air. The birds circle

Rough-legged Hawk
(About 20-22")

and soar in the thermal and let the rising air carry them high into the sky. They use their flight feathers to balance themselves, catching every change in air speed.

Sailplane pilots watch the birds to learn from them where the thermals and up-currents are. Sometimes a pilot circling in a thermal will see three or four Vultures and Hawks soaring beside him. Of course, the birds' feather-covered wings are much more useful in catching the air currents than are the pilot's stiff sailplane wings.

Each species of bird also has its own way of taking flight. Small birds have no trouble getting into the air. When Sparrows are feeding on the ground and something frightens them, they leap into the air and fly away. But big, heavy birds, such as Vultures, have difficulty in doing so. Some run until they have worked up enough speed to take off. Some water birds patter over the surface of the water until they get enough speed to be air-borne. Other water birds, such as Pintail Ducks, spring into the air and fly up at a very steep angle.

Pintail Duck
(26-30")

Birds at Night

Some birds—Quail, for instance—settle down on the ground in a tight little group. Starlings come together in a huge flock at night, calling and chattering to each other as they fly to their roosting places. They make a great clamor before they settle down. Water birds congregate in flocks and float on the water, with their beaks tucked under their wings.

Usually small birds sleep on a limb of a tree or a bush. Their legs and feet muscles enable them to hold on to the branch without staying awake. When the bird puts its weight on its bent legs, the muscles pull the toes down and lock them over the branch. The bird can not unlock its toes until it stands up and straightens its legs, so that the bird can sleep without falling from its perch.

Some species of birds sleep by day and hunt by night. Most Owls are day sleepers. They usually hide in hollow trees or in thick clumps of leaves during the daylight hours.

Chickadees
(4½-5½")

3
Mystery of a Feather

When a bird is flying, its feathers are its sail and its rudder. The feathers provide a raincoat in a storm, an overcoat when the winter winds howl around its perch, and camouflage when the bird wants to hide.

A bird can fluff its feathers in such a way that they stand out from its body and shut in pockets of warm air. That is why a bird may seem much larger than usual on a cold morning. A Chickadee is one of the species of birds that can withstand the winter cold, even when the weather is many degrees below zero.

At night it sits on the limb of a tree and fluffs its feathers down over its toes. Then it tucks its head under its wing. All one can see of a sleeping Chickadee is a little ball of feathers.

Some birds have crests (tufts of feathers on top of their heads) which they can raise or lower. A Blue Jay moves his crest in much the same way as a dog or a mule moves his ears. The bird's crest and the animal's ears seem to show anger, fright, curiosity, or other moods.

Blue Jay
(About 12″)

Birds use feathers to make their nests soft and warm. In the far north, the female Eider Duck plucks her downy feathers from her body. She lays her eggs on a thick blanket of feathers. Whenever the Duck leaves her nest, she pulls the blanket together over the eggs so that it will hide the eggs and keep them warm while the mother Duck is away.

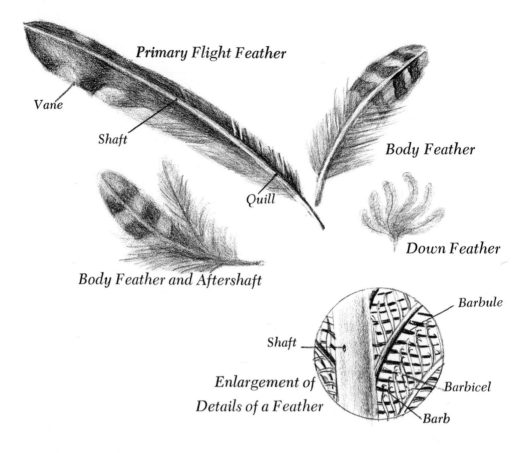

Primary Flight Feather

Vane

Shaft

Quill

Body Feather

Body Feather and Aftershaft

Down Feather

Shaft

Enlargement of
Details of a Feather

Barbule

Barbicel

Barb

A Variety of Feathers

Birds have different kinds of feathers, and each kind serves a different purpose. *Contour feathers* cover most of the body. They are strong, smooth feathers that protect the bird. The center rib of each contour feather is called a *shaft*. On each side of the shaft is a silky, grooved web. This web is called the *vane*.

The vane is made of small rods that lie side by side, running out from the shaft and bending toward the tip of the feather. These little rods are called *barbs*. Each vane has several hundred barbs, which are held together in a flat web by hooks. There are many hundreds of these little hooks on each barb. The hooks on one barb hold on to the ridge in the next barb; they are like miniature zippers, holding the barbs together.

Egret
(38-41")

Snowy Egret
(About 25")

The contour feathers not only cover the body of the bird and give it shape, but they also are the flight feathers. Although the flight feathers are rather stiff and strong, they must bend easily. When a bird is flying, the tips of its wings bend with each stroke. Beneath the contour feathers is a soft, downy undercoat. Down feathers keep birds warm. These feathers hold pockets of air in their fluffy barbs. Ducks and other water birds usually have heavy undercoats of down. Newly-hatched Chickens, Ducks, and Turkeys, Quail, and Pheasants, are covered with soft coats of down when they step out of their shells.

Some feathers are downy near the base and have webs on the tip. Some are as slim as hairs. Other feathers have long curly barbs which make silky plumes. Ostriches and Egrets have such plumes.

Bathing and Preening

Birds take care of their feathers, keeping them in good repair. Some birds have oil glands at the base of their tails. A bird presses the oil gland with its bill, then combs the oil through its feathers as it preens them. Oiling waterproofs the feathers. Some waterfowl experts think that oil glands serve to keep the bills, rather than the feathers, in good condition. There is also evidence that the gland supplies vitamin D. Still other evidence suggests that oil glands are used to keep feathers water-repellent.

Least Flycatcher
(5-6")

Most birds bathe daily. Even in cold weather they try to find water where they can take a quick splash. Some birds sit in the water and fluff their feathers until they are so wet they can scarcely fly. Robins bathe in this way, then flying to a nearby branch, they shake themselves dry. Some birds bathe by taking dashes at the water. Flycatchers swoop down over a pool, splash the water, and fly up again without stopping. Then they sit and preen their feathers.

Many birds bathe by brushing against the dewy grass in the early morning. They fluff their feathers and shake the drops of dew over themselves. Quail, and other birds which belong to the same family as the Chickens, bathe in dust. They roll from one side to the other and kick the dust into their feathers. The dust sifts in next to their skin and helps to kill insect pests. Dusting takes some of the extra oil out of the feathers, too. These birds shake out the dust just as the Robin shakes off the water.

Feathers With Special Uses

Some feathers have special uses. The tail feathers of a Chimney Swift end in sharp spines, which help the Swift to cling to the sides of the chimney where it lives. A Woodpecker also has stiff tail feathers. When it flies to a tree and clings to the bark with its sharp claws, the ends of the stiff tail feathers catch in the bark. The bird leans back on its tail and rests.

A bird's tail is made entirely of feathers. These tail feathers are steering feathers, which are connected with muscles that raise or lower the tail. A bird can spread its tail wide while flying or turning in the air.

Birds use their tails for balancing. Watch a bird perched on a telephone wire. Its tail is moving back and forth constantly, keeping the bird from losing its balance.

Chimney Swift
(5-7″)

The tail is used by almost all birds as a brake. It is pulled downward and spread out into a fanlike shape when the bird is landing.

For most birds the tail serves as a rudder while the bird is in flight. Its function is the same as that of the rudder of an airplane in turning the airplane. Swallows, Terns, and other graceful fliers have long tails which help them to turn quickly to right or left.

The feathers of some birds are harsh and stiff. A Hawk's wings make a whistling sound as it swoops down through the air to catch its prey. Ducks come whistling through the dusk to settle on a pond.

Owls have soft feathers on their wings that make their flight as silent as a shadow. They are not fast fliers, and they can not overtake their victims as the Hawks do. But the Owls' soft feathers make it possible for them to slip up on their prey.

Swallow
(5-7″)

For centuries men have been watching birds and trying to learn from them the secret of air-borne flight. In the year 1000 A.D., according to an English historian, a Benedictine monk made bird-shaped wings and, strapping them to his arms, tried to fly. The first successful glider flight was made in the 1870's by Captain Le Bris, a French sailor, who built his glider with wings shaped like those of an Albatross. The gliders, sailplanes, and airplanes of today have wings shaped somewhat like those of a bird.

The wings of a bird are both wings and propeller. The wings push against the air on every stroke. This movement drives the bird forward. The flight feathers overlap each other. On the down stroke, they present a flat, stiff surface, but when the wing is brought up for the beginning of the next stroke, the feathers separate and let the air through.

Rock Ptarmigan
(About 13")

Autumn

Winter

Willow Ptarmigans
(About 13")

New Feathers for Old

Feathers do not continue to grow after the bird reaches full size. Instead, the whole feather falls out, and a new one grows in its place.

A bird usually grows a complete set of new feathers once a year. Losing the old feathers is called *molting*. Some birds molt twice a year. The winter feathers may be an entirely different color from that of the spring feathers.

Snowy Owl
(About 25″)

Ptarmigans (TAR-mih-ganz) are quail-like birds that live in the snowy regions. In the summer they have mottled brown feathers. If you were to climb the mountains where Ptarmigans live, you might not see them, for they look like the rocks, dry leaves, and grasses around them. When fall comes, the brown feathers fall out, and a new coat of white feathers covers the bird. About the time the Ptarmigan has this new coat, snow falls and again the bird is hard to discover, for it is as white as the snow on which it walks. The Snowy Owl's feathers also change to white in the winter. Each spring it grows a new brown coat.

Feathers Grow in Regular Patterns

There are one hundred and thirty-four species of Owls throughout the world, but only eighteen in North America. One is small as a Sparrow and the largest has a wingspread of about five feet. Scientists say that each Owl has twelve steering feathers in its tail and eleven primary flight feathers in each wing.

American Bittern
(About 24″)

A bird molts its feathers in a regular pattern too. Usually the large wing feathers fall out in pairs. The bird loses the outside feathers on each wing at the same time and then it loses the next one on each side. In this way the bird's wings are always in balance. Its tail feathers usually fall out in the same way, one on each side at the same time.

Some water birds lose all their flight feathers at once and can not fly for several weeks. They find food and escape their enemies by swimming and hiding among the weeds during the molting season.

Feathers Help Birds Hide

Many birds are brightly colored, and others have feathers whose colors imitate those of their surroundings. A Bittern stands straight and slim, pointing its bill toward the sky. It looks very much like a dry, broken reed.

Most young shore birds and Gulls are speckled, much like the ground on which they live. They so closely resemble a clod of earth that it is difficult for their enemies to find them. Many brightly-colored birds blend in with their surroundings. Some Warblers look like yellow leaves. Even black-and-white Woodpeckers resemble the light and shadows on a tree trunk.

Ruddy Turnstone
(About 9″)

4
Bills, Bills, Bills

A bird's bill is its best food-getting tool. A bird often carries its food with its bill. The Gulls, water birds that live by lakes and oceans, snatch the clams in their bills and fly into the air with them. They drop the clams on a rocky beach to break the shells, and then dive down and eat the meaty food.

A Jay drives a nut into a forked branch where it can pry the nut open with its bill. Some Woodpeckers wedge acorns into rough places in the bark of a tree so that they can peel off the hull. Other Woodpeckers dig holes in wood with their bills to hold the acorns while they are eating.

Nuthatches have weak, small bills. This bird looks for a crevice in the bark just large enough to hold a piece of nut that it may have picked up.

A bird uses its bill to find food. Roadrunners which live on the ground, turn over pieces of caked mud with their bills to uncover the insects beneath. Shore birds, such as Turnstones, flip over stones and sticks with their strong bills as they feed along the beach. Then they gobble up the insects or the small crabs hiding there.

Sanderlings, a species of small shore birds, have weak, little bills. Since they can not turn over the stones themselves, they follow right at the tails of the Turnstones. Any insects that escape the bigger birds are snatched by the Sanderlings.

The Snipe, a bird of wet meadows and marshes, has an extremely long bill, with soft, flexible tips. These adaptations allow the bird to probe for insects and worms that live in the mud.

Roadrunner
(About 25″)

Most birds' bills are horny and hard. Some birds stab their prey. A Great Blue Heron, one of the largest birds in America, settles down on a pond and stands quietly in the water. As soon as a fish or frog comes close, out shoots the Heron's long neck. It stabs the frog or fish with its slim, sharp bill.

White Pelicans
(About 60")

Pelicans have queer bills. These big water birds have large lower beaks which can be expanded into a deep pouch. Swimming through the water, a Pelican scoops up several fish at one time. It lets the water run out of its bill and keeps the fish in its pouch. The Pelican may take the fish to its young ones or swallow it.

Sanderling
(About 6″)

Snipe
(10-11″)

A bird's bill is its tool for building a home as well as for catching food. A Woodpecker drills a hole in a tree for its home. When the hole is large enough, the Woodpecker smooths the inside of it and then lines the nesting cavity with fine chips.

Bushtit
(About 4½″)

Oriole
(About 7″)

Bushtits, among the smallest of American birds, build their nest on a leafy branch that hangs down free from other leaves and limbs. The nest is in the form of a hanging basket and is at least three times as long as the birds themselves. The Bushtits weave a fine web of cobwebs and plant fibers—a web so thin that one can see the bird working inside. One of the pair stays in the basket nest, weaving and smoothing the material with its bill. The mate makes hundreds of trips across the fields, bringing back plant fibers in its bill and passing them in through a small opening at the top of the web. The outside of the nest is decorated with bits of lichens held on by spider webs.

Orioles build long hanging nests, also. They weave the fibers in and out with their sharp bills. A farmer's wife found a young Oriole that had fallen from the nest. Since the bird was raised in the house, it never saw another Oriole. But the next spring, when nesting time came, it began to weave. It took threads from the sewing basket and sewed the window curtains together. It poked the thread through the material with its bill; then it went around to the other side and pulled the thread through. It was sewing the curtain into a nest—a case of instinct (untaught behavior) against the environment!

A bird's bill gives a good clue to what a bird eats. The Hummingbird's extremely long bill allows it to reach into a flower and sip the nectar. The Hawk catches and eats birds and other small animals, using its thick, strong bill to tear apart its food. Swifts, Nighthawks, Swallows, and Flycatchers feed while flying. They dart and skim through the air, with their enormous short-billed mouths wide open, scooping up the insects.

Nighthawk
(8-10″)

Red Crossbill
(5½-6½″)

Swallow
(5-7″)

Wild Canary or Goldfinch
(4-6″)

Birds that belong to the Sparrow-Finch family are seed-eaters. They crack seeds with their thick, strong, cone-shaped bills. A Canary is a species of Finch. Watch a Canary eating. It turns the seeds quickly in its bill and snips off the hard shell just as its wild Finch and Sparrow cousins do.

Crossbills, too, belong to the Finch family. The birds pry up the scales of the pine cones with their strange, crossed bills and pick out the pine nuts with their shovel-like tongues. This is the only way a Crossbill can get its food. Because of its odd-shaped bill, it can not pick up food from the ground.

Most Ducks have scoop-shaped bills with which they scoop up insects. Some Ducks have fringed edges, like little teeth, on their bills. These fringes allow the water to drain away, leaving only the food. If you watch Ducks on a pond, you will see them paddling around in the shallow water, stirring up the mud and insects from the bottom of the pond. Then you will see them reach into the water and scoop up the food.

Great Blue Heron
(About 52")

5
Feet Are Clues

Sometimes in the mud along a stream, you may see a bird track as big as your hand. The toe tracks are very long and slim. Since the tracks are far apart, you know at once that a big bird with long legs made them. If you watch quietly, you may see the bird—a Great Blue Heron. The tracks may lead down the shore and into the water, for the Heron is a wading bird.

Sandpiper
(7-9″)

It is interesting to study bird tracks in the dust of the road or on the muddy bank of a stream and try to guess what kind of bird made each track.

Along the edge of the pond, the large, webbed feet of Ducks make three-cornered tracks. On the beach, the delicate feet of the Sandpipers leave spidery tracks that run in and out among the driftwood.

Baldpate Duck
(18-22″)

Quail make neat tracks as they walk in the dusty road, setting each foot down in front of the other. Pigeons make interesting tracks, too, each track directly in front of the other, with the toes turned inward—pigeon-toed.

Ducks, Geese, Gulls, and most other water birds, have webbed feet. Their feet are efficient paddles that push through the water at a fast rate. The webbing between their toes helps these birds to walk on the mud at the water's edge.

Gallinules are chicken-like birds that live near the water, especially in marshes. These birds have yellow or greenish legs and feet. The birds skip across the water from one lily pad to the next. Gallinules have long, slender toes and long toenails.

Gallinules
(About 14")

Least Flycatcher
(5-6″)

Crested Flycatcher
(8-9″)

These enable them to distribute their weight evenly on the thin lily leaves in the same way that snowshoes distribute a person's weight on the soft snow.

Perching Birds

Most of our familiar land birds of North America belong to the great order of perching birds. Usually these birds have four toes on each foot; three toes turn forward and one turns backward. They also have rather long toenails. These birds can perch on a tree, lock their toes over the branch and go to sleep without danger of falling.

Red-bellied Woodpecker
(About 10″)

Red-headed Woodpecker
(8½-9½″)

Birds of this order have many different ways of using their perching feet. Some of them spend much time on the ground scratching for food. Sparrows belong to the order of perching birds. They are seed-eating birds, and many of them scratch among the fallen leaves, hunting for seeds. Their strong feet and long toenails send the leaves flying.

Other perching birds do not hunt for food while on the ground. Flycatchers and Swallows catch insects while flying, although they have perching feet to hold them on the tree limbs when resting.

Pecking Birds

The Woodpecker does not belong to the order of perching birds. It is a pecking bird. It seldom perches on a limb—its feet are adapted for clinging. Most Woodpeckers have four toes, but

51

they are arranged differently from those of perching birds. The first and fourth toes point backwards, and the second and third toes point forward. This arrangement of the toes helps the Woodpecker to cling to the bark of a tree trunk. The bird then can turn either way and reach out for its food, and its strong toes will keep it from falling.

Bobwhite
(9½-10¾″)

Scratching Birds

Chickens and Turkeys are scratching birds. Quail, Pheasants, and Grouse are wild birds belonging to this same bird order. All these birds have three toes which point forward. The

Turkeys
(36-48″)

Ruffed Grouse
(16-19″)

hind toe is very short and is raised above the ground. In this way, the bird can scratch without the toes getting in the way.

The Grouse lives in snowy country. In the winter, it grows long feathers on its feet. These resemble snowshoes that allow the bird to walk on the snow without sinking into the deep drifts.

Horned Owl
(About 25″)

Bald Eagle
(About 37″)

Birds of Prey

The grasping feet of Hawks, Eagles, and Owls show that these are birds of prey. The four toes are evenly spaced and end in long nails that curve into fierce talons. These birds drop down out of the air, clutch their prey, and carry the food to their nests.

Vultures, although they are birds of prey, do not have strong feet with curved talons. The Vultures are scavengers, eaters of dead animals. Since these birds do not catch their prey, their feet are rather small with short toenails.

Osprey
(21-24½")

Herring Gull
(About 26")

Laughing Gull
(About 17")

6

Birds' Nest

Male Robins arrive in the spring, two or three weeks before the female birds. Each Robin looks over the trees and shrubs until he finds the place where he wants to spend the summer. He defends this place against all other Robins, even to the point of fighting for it.

Barn Swallows build their bottle-shaped mud nests as close together as they can stick them. The air is their feeding ground, and they have no need to guard a strip of territory. They swoop together here and there, gathering insects over rivers and lakes.

The Gulls lay their eggs close together in colonies on some rocky islands. These birds also have a wide feeding territory.

Quail
(9-10")

Veery
(About 7½")

Oceans or lakes are the Gulls' hunting grounds, therefore there is no reason for them to hunt alone.

Habitat

Birds choose various locations or niches. Some nests will be on the ground and others will be in the top of the tallest tree. Among the birds that nest on the ground are Meadowlarks, Whip-poor-wills, Veery, Quail, Nighthawks, and Woodcocks.

Whip-poor-will
(9-10¼")

Woodcock
(10½-11¾")

Song Sparrow
(5-6")

Goldfinch
(4½-6")

In the low shrubs and undergrowth you may expect to find the nests of Catbirds, Maryland Yellowthroats, Brown Towhees, Goldfinches, Song Sparrows, and some of the small Flycatchers. Many kinds of Warblers prefer the low shrubs.

Brown Towhee
(8½-10")

Catbird
(About 9")

Oriole
(About 8″)

Purple Finch
(5½-6½″)

Vireos, Cardinals, Mourning Doves, Robins, House Wrens, Chipping Sparrows, Jays, and Thrushes are some of the birds that find their niches in the middle branches of trees. Higher in the trees swing the nests of the Orioles. Purple Finches and many Warblers nest there, too. Hawks and Eagles nest in the highest branches of trees.

Many species of birds, most commonly the Woodpeckers, nest in holes of trees. Bluebirds, Chickadees, Titmice, and Nut-hatches nest in holes, also. Since these small birds have weak bills, most of them can not dig out the nesting hole themselves. Instead, they search for old Woodpecker holes or knotholes in trees. Owls, too, nest in natural cavities in trees. One species, however, the Burrowing Owl, lives in holes in the ground. This bird chooses a hole which has been dug by a ground squirrel or a prairie dog. In fact, the Owl sometimes joins these animals in occupying the nesting hole.

Cardinal
(About 9½″)

Vireo
(5-6″)

Chipping Sparrow
(About 5″)

Wren
(4½-5″)

Robin
(About 10″)

Hermit Thrush
(6-7″)

Bluebird
(6-7½″)

Titmouse
(5½-6½″)

Species Build Alike

Birds that belong to the same species build alike. A bird knows how to build its first nest without being taught, and that is the only kind of nest it can ever build.

Nests on the Ground

The Meadowlark lives in meadows and open fields. If the grass is tall, the Meadowlark weaves it into a dome over the nest. If it is short, the bird brings in grass and makes a covering. Since the nest is on the ground, a prowling animal or bird could see the eggs from above, were it not for this covering. This bird can also build a grass-covered tunnel to slip unseen to the nest.

Meadowlark
(About 9")

Burrowing Owl
(About 9")

One day we saw a Meadowlark drop down into the field and disappear. Quietly we began to hunt for the nest which was sure to be hidden nearby. Soon we found the little covered walkway leading through the grass, and at the end of the tunnel was the Meadowlark's nest.

The Nighthawk makes its home on bare, sandy ground or gravel. This bird hides its eggs by making no nest at all. The eggs, dull in color, are speckled with dark markings and look very much like the gravel on which they are laid. A nest of grass or leaves would be conspicuous.

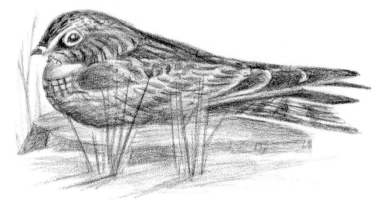

Nighthawk
(8-10")

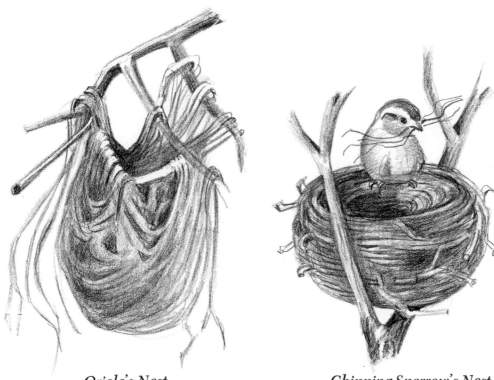

Oriole's Nest

Chipping Sparrow's Nest

Woodpecker's Nest

Catbird's Nest

63

Ringed Plover
(About 7")

Killdeer
(About 11")

A Killdeer's favorite nesting place is also on gravel bars and the eggs look much like pieces of water-worn granite, such as you find in a creek bed. We almost stepped on a set of eggs which were right in the middle of a gravel road that ran through the meadow. Of course, there was neither a straw nor a leaf in this nesting place.

Water birds usually build their nests near a stream or a lake so that the young birds can take to the water as soon as they are hatched. The handsome, brightly-colored Wood Duck nests in a hole in the trunk of a tree. When the little "woodies" are hatched, they tumble from the nesting hole to the ground. They are such light balls of down that the fall does not hurt them. The mother then leads them to the nearest pond.

Horned Grebes
(12-15″)

Grebes, a species of water birds, build a floating raft of water plants for a nest. The birds pull up stalks and roots of plants to form a floating island. This they anchor to the reeds by loops of plant material.

Instinct has taught the birds not to fasten the nest firmly to the plants. Should the water rise, a tightly-fastened nest would tip over and spill the eggs. But the nest that is loosely fastened will ride up and down with the waves and with the rising and lowering water. These floating rafts are not used as homes for the young birds. As soon as the Grebes are out of the shell, they slip off the nest and swim away.

Most birds use a nest for only one season. Eagles, however, usually occupy their nests year after year. They add material to

Red-tailed Hawk
(22-25″)

the nest each spring until it becomes a great heap of sticks. An Eagle's nest usually sits in the top of the tallest tree in the neighborhood or on the spreading arms of a dead tree.

Red-tailed Hawks also build big nests and add to them each year. Often the Hawk's nest will be on the top of a dead stub.

7

Young Birds

Different birds lay a different number of eggs. A Condor, the great Vulture of California, nests every other year and lays only one egg during that period. Other birds, such as the Quail, lay fifteen eggs or more.

Eggs laid by birds of the same species are shaped alike. Some birds lay eggs that are as round as marbles. Eggs that are shaped rather like a top, with one end much smaller than the other, will not roll. Birds that nest on cliffs and rocky ledges usually lay eggs of this shape.

Gamble's Quail
(10-11")

Eggs can be identified by the way they are marked and by the color. Some eggs are spotted; others have scroll marks all over them. Some are blue, some brown, some green, and some are plain white.

After the eggs are laid, the mother begins to incubate them. In some species the father bird will take his turn in incubating; in a few species, the father never comes near the nest. The female Hummingbird builds her nest, incubates the eggs, and does the feeding of the young birds all by herself.

When the baby bird in the shell has grown until it fills all the space, it begins to peck its way out. With its bill it makes a break in the shell. The bird keeps pecking until it has made a series of breaks all the way around the egg. Suddenly it gives an extra push and the end of the egg falls away. The young bird struggles out into the nest.

Some birds are helpless when newly-hatched. Their eyes are closed and their bodies are nearly naked. All they can do is raise their heads on wobbly necks and open their mouths wide. The parents bring food and shove it down their throats.

Most birds are almost void of feathers when hatched. Hummingbirds, for instance, look like insects or worms, for they are completely naked. But in just a day or two, feathers begin to sprout through the skin. The young birds grow remarkably fast. In ten days or two weeks they are fully covered with feathers and are as wide awake as can be. Many of the small species of birds are about ready to leave the nest and fly in two weeks.

Some species of birds can run almost as soon as they are hatched. Their bodies are covered with a soft coat of fluffy down. Chicks and Ducklings belong to this class of bird, as do young Quail and Pheasants. The parents of these young birds lead the young ones and show them where the food is, and the birds pick it up from the ground.

Learning to Fly

The young of birds that nest in trees must be able to fly in order to leave the home. As soon as their wings are feathered, they start practicing flying.

A young bird will hold on to the edge of the nest with its feet and flutter its wings just as though it were flying. Hummingbirds vibrate their wings until they make a humming sound. Their wings lift them clear out of the nest, while their feet cling to the edge. The young birds practice in this way for several days.

When the time comes to leave, some birds are too timid to make the dive from the nest. The parents will call and coax, trying to persuade them to launch out into the air. When the young do leave, they scatter and light in trees and shrubbery near the nesting tree. The parents hurry from one to the other, feeding them. Soon the young birds are following the parents as they fly.

Instinct

Young birds have a built-in means of protection. This is the instinct to obey. *Instinct* is an inborn quality in animals or in human beings that enables them to do something without being taught.

Prairie Hen
(About 17")

Most young birds are with their parents for only a short time—not long enough for the parents to teach the young birds what they need to know about preserving their lives. Actually, from the moment the birds are hatched, they have the instinct of self-preservation. For example, they already know what their parents' calls mean and how to obey them. As soon as the mother calls, the young bird obeys.

One day out in the woods, we saw newly-hatched Quail obey commands they had never heard before. We had been watching a Quail's nest that was near a wood road. We wanted to take pictures of the young ones before they left the nest. To do this, we would have to be there the very morning they hatched.

One evening when we stopped by the nest we heard a faint peeping coming from the eggs. This meant that the next morning there would be young Quail in the nest.

Early the next morning we set up our camera several feet from the nest. The mother did not want to leave, but finally she slipped from the nest. There, huddled close together, were twelve fluffy Quail. They were tan with stripes of darker brown.

The mother gave a soft call, and the young birds tumbled out of the nest and ran on wobbly legs toward her. She led them a few feet away and then she gave another call. This meant a different command, for each little bird stopped right where it was and sank down on the pine needles.

It seemed to us that every one of the twelve birds had disappeared. Actually, the Quail looked so much like the pine needles and leaves that they were hidden as long as they did not move.

Young Killdeer hide themselves in the same way—by being perfectly still. When the mother calls, they squat on the ground

Sandpiper
(7-9")

and stretch out their heads against the earth. When they do this, they are almost invisible, for their white throats are hidden.

Birds that can run as soon as they are hatched seem to have this protection of obeying by instinct. Young Sandpipers and other shore birds are quick to obey. Ducklings, also, belong to this class of young. When danger threatens, a mother Duck will hide her babies among the reeds. She gives a soft quack which seems to mean "stay hidden," and then she swims away. The little birds stay right where the mother left them until she returns.

Redhead
Duck

Wood Duck

Pintail Duck

Mallard Duck

Mergansers

Snow Goose

Golden-winged Warbler

Hooded Warbler

Cedar Waxwing
(6½-8")

8
Songs and Calls

Some species of birds have a great variety of calls, and others utter only a single note. The Cedar Waxwing has only one note, a high whistle. We have in a cage a Waxwing with a broken wing. The cage is small and the bird can not try to fly. We hope the wing will heal. Meanwhile, it lives on the wild berries we pick for it. Although it whistles only one note, it has many different ways of expressing itself. Sometimes at dusk it whistles a plaintive "Ssssst!" At other times, when we are near and it is feeling companionable, the whistled note is a trill, a glad sound. When we forget to put berries in the cage, the bird's call is loud and reproachful. When a flock of Waxwings come to the bird-bath in the yard, the cry of our injured bird seems full of anguish—it so wants to join its fellows.

Hooded Warbler
(5-6")

Hermit Thrush
(6-7")

Those who have studied bird calls say that the Crow has a greater variety of calls than any other bird. The leader of the flock appears to be a wise old bird that directs the flock with caws and calls.

In winter when birds travel in flocks, there is much calling among them. The soft talk of a flock of Quail is pleasant to hear. Flocks of migrating Geese keep together by honking. Sometimes the leader honks, and the call is repeated from one to the other until it ripples from the front to the end of the long line.

Almost all perching birds, such as Warblers, Thrushes, and Sparrows, have a song in addition to their calls. Usually it is the male birds that sing. Most female birds have only soft calls and trills.

Each species of bird can be recognized by the song, for each has a distinctive song, a phrase, or a melody of its own. Some-

Chickadee
(4½-5½")

Bobolink
(6¼-8")

times there is a slight difference between the singing of individual birds. Some have finer voices than others. In our yard live three Song Sparrows, each in its own territory. Their songs are easily recognized as Song Sparrow tunes, yet each bird's way of singing is slightly different.

Some birds are named for their songs. The cheerful "chickadee-dee-dee" has given the Chickadees their name. "Bobwhite" is an interpretation of the call of this well-known bird.

"Flicker, flicker, flicker," is what the call of the brown Woodpecker sounds like, and it has given the Flicker its name.

If you have ever disturbed a Killdeer in the meadow and have heard its "kill-dee-dee-dee" as it flies, you will know where this bird's name came from. The Whip-poor-will is named for its calls; and the mewing call of the Catbird is familiar to many.

Although most species of birds have their own songs, a few birds can sing the songs of others. The Mockingbird does just what its name implies—it mimics the songs of other birds and even of other animals. It will sing like a Robin, whistle like a Cardinal, shift to the harsh calls of the Jay, mew like a cat, crow like a Rooster, and whine like a puppy, all in one song.

It can imitate other sounds as well. When camping with a group of students, we heard the leader's police whistle. When

Mockingbird
(About 10¼″)

Catbird
(About 9″)

we obeyed the call, the leader was surprised because he had not whistled. Suddenly, we heard the call again. Of course, it was a Mockingbird that lived in the tree over the leader's tent. The bird had learned a new sound to add to its accomplishments.

How birds sing is more easily explained than sung. They have a voice box called a *syrinx*. In many birds, the syrinx can produce rolling trills, soft notes, whistles, and other sounds that make up the song of a bird. In order to recognize bird songs, it is necessary to analyze them. Some songs are a single note, like the Waxwing's song. Others trill on one note. Some songs rise and fall with a melody. Some calls are twitterings, like the calls of the Swallows.

The song of the Bobolink is a rollicking, bubbling one; the call of the Owl is soft and deep. One of the deepest and most far-reaching of all songs is the "who-oo-oo" of the Great Horned Owl. It is a sound that makes you burrow deeper into your sleeping bag when you hear it in the woods. Doves have soft, sad-sounding voices. One of the most common sounds in the spring in most parts of the United States is the plaintive call of the Mourning Dove. The Dove repeats the song hundreds of times a day.

Red-throated Loon
(About 24")

Common Loon
(About 35")

Loons are large water birds that have weird calls. They sound like crazy laughter, as their calls ring out over a lonely lake at dusk. People, who do not know it is a bird calling, are often frightened by the "ha-a-a-a-a-a."

Perhaps one of the most thrilling sounds in nature is the great trumpeting call of the wild Swan. The Trumpeter Swan, the largest of all the water birds, has a call like the sound of a brass horn. The call of the slightly smaller Whistling Swan might be compared to two notes played on a clarinet. When a flock of Swans is passing overhead, the notes float down from the sky like a silvery chorus.

Ruby-throated Hummingbird
(3-3¼″)

9
The Great Travel Adventure

There are three hundred and nineteen species of Humming-birds in the world. Although eighteen are found in North America, one species only inhabits the United States east of Texas and the Rocky Mountains. This is the Ruby-throated Hummingbird. This species weighs much less than an ounce. Yet it is one of the great travelers in the bird world. When the bird has stored up fat in its body it starts south on its journey.

Its destination may be Florida, Mexico, or Central America. How it reaches Central America, we are not sure. Some scientists think that it leaves the southern states and flies straight across the Gulf of Mexico. This would mean that it would have to fly five hundred miles without stopping to rest or to feed. It would be out of sight of land all the way and would be guided only by its sense of direction.

Some say that this journey is impossible for a Humming-bird, and that the bird flies south following the gulf coast around through Texas. It is probable that some of the Ruby-throats go by way of the coast and some cross the water. Whichever way they travel, it is a remarkable journey for a bird weighing less than a penny. And Hummingbirds do not travel in flocks; each jewel-like bird flashes off by itself.

This great journey is called *migration*. Many species of birds migrate. Some of them cover vast distances, and others go only a few hundred miles. For centuries men have been curious about the travels of the birds. They have wondered where the birds went in the fall and how they spent the winter.

Swallows were observed in Europe, leaving in great flocks in the fall and returning in the spring. It was thought that the birds hibernated, slept, all winter; that they flew into mud banks and buried themselves for the winter. In 1740, a man by the name of Frisch decided to find out whether this theory was true.

Swallows
(5½-7½")

Phoebe
(About 7½")

He tied red threads on the legs of some Swallows, with the idea that if the birds did spend the winter buried in mud, the threads would be muddy and discolored by spring. When he caught the birds on their return the following May, the threads were still fairly bright. Mr. Frisch felt reasonably sure that the hibernation theory was untrue.

Birdbanding

As a boy, John James Audubon, the famous bird artist, lived on a farm in Pennsylvania. He watched some Phoebes nesting along the creek. When fall came and the birds flew away, he wondered if the same birds would come back in the spring. The next year, when there were young birds in the Phoebes' nests, he made little bands of silver wire and fastened them around the ankles of five birds. They were still wearing their silver bracelets when they flew away in the fall.

Audubon waited eagerly for the Phoebes to return in the spring. At last a little flock of birds arrived and began to build their nests along the stream. Two of the Phoebes were wearing silver bands. Thus Audubon had proved that Phoebes return to the same place where they were hatched. He was satisfied that birds do fly a regular path.

Nearly a hundred years passed before any record was made of birdbanding. In 1901 several ornithologists (OR-nih-THOLL-uh-jists), those who study birds, began using little metal bands to mark birds. Imprinted on the bands were the words, "Return to Smithsonian." Many people who found the marked birds returned the bands to the Smithsonian Institution in Washington, D.C. The bands helped the ornithologists to know where the birds had gone on their long travels.

Now, thousands of birds are banded every year. Young Ducks, for instance, are marked at their nesting grounds, and the bands are returned when the birds are shot by hunters on the winter feeding range. Some of the bands are removed thousands of miles from the spot where they were clamped on the Ducklings' legs.

Flyways

For many years no one really knew the paths the birds followed as they migrated. Then ornithologists began to study the records of banded birds. If the band was returned, a record was made of where the bird had been banded and where it was found. The ornithologists marked the two places on their maps and drew a line between the two dots. This line showed the path the bird probably traveled. As more and more lines were drawn, a definite pattern developed. The birds were following paths in the sky. Ornithologists called these paths *flyways*.

Four great flyways lead the migrating birds across North America in spring and in fall. Usually the birds follow the same paths on both trips.

The Atlantic Flyway leads the birds from Greenland, New England, and Canada. This flyway takes them south along the coast to Florida. Some birds continue on to the West Indies and to South America.

The Mississippi Flyway brings the birds down from the shores of Hudson Bay and the central plains of Canada. Some birds from the Yukon and northern Alaska follow this route. For the majority, the journey ends along the Gulf of Mexico. Millions of birds congregate along the coastal marshes from Texas to Florida.

The Mississippi Flyway is the most popular of any of the paths. It is easy to understand why. No mountains bar the way, and there are well-watered valleys for rest and feeding.

The Central Flyway is a path for the land birds of the Rocky Mountain regions and for the waterfowl of the great plains. From the Mackenzie Delta on the shores of the Arctic Ocean and from northern Alaska come millions of waterfowl. Pintail Ducks, Redhead Ducks, and Baldpate Ducks are chief among the migrants on this flyway.

Sandhill Cranes
(About 44")

Redhead Ducks
(18-22″)

Pintail Duck
(26-30″)

Baldpate Duck
(18-22″)

Canada Goose
(32-40")

Snow Goose
(23-28")

The Pacific Flyway brings the birds from Alaska, western Canada, and the western side of the Rocky Mountains. Countless numbers of Snow Geese, Whistling Swans, Canada Geese, and Sandhill Cranes follow this path. Great flocks of Ducks also use the Pacific Flyway. Many of them go no farther than the grain fields and swamps of California. A few of the water birds and many land birds fly down the Pacific coast until they reach Central America and South America.

Bobolink
(6¼-8″)

Bobolink's Journey

The Bobolink is a yellow, black, and white bird of the open fields. It is found in the eastern and central states, where it spends its summer. In the fields and meadows, it sings its bubbling song, making it a favorite with all. As summer draws to a close, the bright tips of its feathers wear away, and it becomes a plain tan bird streaked with brown. With other Bobolinks, it flies to the rice fields and marshes of the southern states. There they settle down to feast on rice and wild grapes. Some people call the Bobolink the Ricebird. When they are fat and round, these birds are ready for the next part of their journey.

The Bobolinks fly across the Gulf of Mexico to Cuba and Jamaica. From these islands, they cross the open sea for four hundred miles. When they reach the shores of South America, their journey is not yet ended, for the country is covered with great jungles. Bobolinks eat weed seeds and insects, which they find in the open field. They can not live in the jungles, so they must keep on flying over jungles until they reach the fields and marshes of southern Brazil.

At this point in their journey, the birds are south of the equator, and are flying into springtime, even though it is November. The birds of Brazil are busy building their nests. But this is vacation time for the Bobolinks from North America.

They spend the next few months rollicking over the fields and enjoying the long summer days.

By May, the Bobolinks have their new coats of feathers. The males are again yellow, black, and white. They gather in flocks for the long journey back north. In June, they are again nesting in the meadows where they were hatched.

Hooded Warbler
(5-6″)

Wilson's Warbler
(5-5¾″)

Ovenbird
(5½-6″)

Warblers are small, shy birds, whose feather coats are quite thin. They are really birds of the tropics, and they spend two-thirds of the year in the forests of Central and South America. It is strange that such small, frail birds should take so long and dangerous a journey. Warblers do so each spring, when they fly north and spread over North America from Texas to Alaska.

Except for Owls and Nighthawks, one usually thinks of birds as being active during the daytime. But most of the small birds, including the Warblers, make their migratory journey in the night. They feed all day and then start their long flight just after dark. How far they fly in a night is not known. If they fly over land, the journey is not so great. If they fly over water, they must keep flying until they reach the distant shores.

Many of the birds that follow the Central Flyway cross the Great Lakes on their way to Canada. Flying over water is dangerous for land birds. Not only is there no place for resting, but the weather also may cause many birds to lose their lives. If a heavy wind blows against them, they may become too tired to reach land. Then they will fly lower and lower until they are caught by the waves. Sometimes a late snowstorm in the spring catches the first migrants. A snowstorm over Lake Michigan during the migration will kill thousands of small birds.

Water Birds

Water birds find migrating easier than do the land birds. They can stop and rest on the water. The Arctic Tern, a fifteen-inch gray bird with a forked tail, black cap and a red bill, is a champion distance flyer. It flies from the top of the world to the bottom and back again each year—a round trip of more than twenty-five thousand miles!

This little, gull-like Tern builds its nest on the mosses that grow over the frozen earth in the north. There, the sun shines all day and night during the summer months, and the tundras swarm with insects. It is an ideal place for Terns to nest.

When the short summer comes to an end and the sun begins to dip below the horizon at midnight, the Arctic Terns become restless. It is time for them to begin their journey. They fly south for thousands of miles until they come to the Antarctic. The Terns, by taking this long migratory journey, spend more than half their lives under the midnight sun.

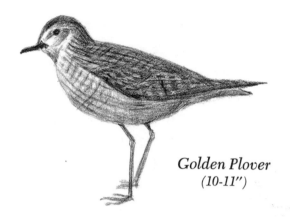

Golden Plover
(10-11")

Shore Birds

Another famous migrant is the Golden Plover, one of the shore birds. Its journey is even more remarkable than that of the Tern, for it does not feed on the water. It is the belief of many scientists that this bird does not even light on the water to rest.

The Golden Plover nests north of the Arctic Circle. When the young are able to care for themselves, the parents leave them and start on their journey to the pampas, plains of Argentina. The journey takes the Plovers southeast through Labrador and Nova Scotia. Directly to the south lies the broad Atlantic Ocean, but the Plovers, without hesitating, take off for the two-thousand-mile flight. No one knows how long the flight takes, but Plovers are swift flyers. If they meet a storm, their journey is filled with danger.

Stranger yet is the journey of the young Plovers. After the parents leave, the young birds gather into flocks. Soon they, also, start for the grassy plains of Argentina. But the young birds do not follow the route their parents took. They fly south, down through the central part of the continent, following the Mississippi Flyway. They fly over Central America, across the Andes Mountains, and on to their resting and feeding grounds,where they join the flocks of older birds.

How the young birds find the way, no one knows. Bird watchers have not reported seeing a parent bird with the young ones, nor have they reported a young bird traveling south with the parent birds.

In the spring, the Golden Plovers return to the Arctic together. They follow the route the young birds took in the fall, crossing the Andes and flying along the Pacific Ocean coastline to Panama. Then they fly on up through Central America, where the route takes them through the Mississippi Valley and on to the far north.

The Pacific Golden Plovers, which nest along the west coast of Alaska, follow another route. They fly across two thousand miles of ocean to the Hawaiian Islands. It is beyond our understanding how the birds find these small islands in the vast expanse of ocean. But year after year, the same birds return to the same islands. One bird with a crippled leg returned for a number of years to the lonely little island of Midway.

That shore birds, which seldom swim or alight on the water, are able to make such long flights across the ocean seems almost unbelievable. When they follow the great flyways, birds show a sense of direction far superior to man's.

White Ibis
(About 27")

10

Wildlife Refuges

Millions of water birds build their nests in the tundras and swamps of the far north. They nest along the Bering Sea, on the delta of the Yukon River, along the great swamps of the Mackenzie River. They spread over thousands of square miles that are seldom visited by man.

This far north country provides just what the water and shore birds need as a summer home. There is daylight almost all the time, and since the air is full of insects, food for the birds is plentiful. But when the nights become longer and winter begins to chill the land, the birds turn toward the south.

For centuries these migratory flights have been carried on. Some of the birds found the food and shelter they needed during the winter in the swamps of the West; others flew to the marshlands along the Atlantic Ocean. But the greatest number of birds came down the center of North America to the marshes along the Mississippi River, where they settled in enormous flocks on the shores of the Gulf of Mexico.

When the pioneers came, the country changed. Miles of marshes were drained. Some of the land was plowed and made into farms. The rivers that had spread out into vast swamps in the winter were kept in their channels. The birds that came south could not find enough lakes or rivers to live on.

There were hunters waiting to kill the birds, too. Hundreds of thousands of wildfowl were shot each year. They were shot as they flew south in the fall; they were hunted on their winter feeding grounds; they were shot as they returned north in the spring.

After many years people began to realize that there were not nearly as many Ducks and Geese as before. Something had to be done about saving the birds. Government men began to study the flyways that the Ducks and Geese traveled. Unlike mammals, whose feet mark the earth, the birds left no record of their passing. No one knew just where they came from or where they went. When men began banding the birds and studying the records of the bands that were returned, they found out where the birds traveled.

Then the government began to buy back some of the swamps and lands that had been drained. The lands were flooded again so that the water birds could have homes and food. The first lands to be turned into wildlife refuges were in Oregon and California along the Pacific Flyways. When the swamps of Malheur Lake and of Lower Klamath Lake in Oregon were flooded, birds began to stop there, as they had before the lakes had been drained.

Whooping Cranes
(About 50")

All across the United States on the great flyways, the government made refuges where birds could rest and feed. On some of the refuges, flocks of birds rested and then flew on. Other refuges were used as winter feeding grounds. Year after year, more areas have been set aside as refuges. Some of these areas are protected because they are the homes of rare birds. Along the coast of Texas is the Aransas National Wildlife Refuge. It is the winter home of the rarest bird in the world, the Whooping Crane.

Aransas National Wildlife Refuge

A hundred years ago, Whooping Cranes nested in the marshes of Louisiana and on up through the central states. Today, not one nests in the United States. For years it was not known where the Whooping Cranes were nesting. They left the Aransas Refuge in the spring and disappeared toward the north. A few years ago, bird watchers in an airplane saw tall white birds on the shores of Great Slave Lake in Canada. When they reported this, government men made a trip into the isolated tundras and swamps. There they found a little colony of nesting Cranes. This wild place was the goal of their twenty-five-hundred-mile flight from Texas.

Once thousands of these great, snow-white birds flew on black-tipped wings through the sky. On they flew to their nesting grounds in the central states and on to the Arctic Circle. Their wild, bugling cries were familiar music to the pioneers. Many of the great birds were shot. When their winter feeding grounds were destroyed, the birds had no place to live.

Now there are only a few Whooping Cranes in the whole world. Perhaps, if these few are cared for and protected, there will some day be larger flocks. Sometimes a few young birds return from the north with the thirty or more adults each fall; other years there seem to be no young birds. Perhaps it is too late to save these birds from extinction. One spring the last Whooping Crane may fly north never to return.

Ross' Goose
(About 23″)

Sacramento Wildlife Refuge

The Sacramento Wildlife Refuge in California is the winter home of the smallest Goose, the Ross' Goose. These small Geese, not much larger than Mallard Ducks, nest along the Perry River on the Arctic coast, east of the Mackenzie Delta. Each fall, they fly diagonally across Canada in a southwesterly direction. In November they arrive at the refuge in California. Here they are carefully protected.

Millions of other water birds share the refuge. Cackling Geese, a small relative of the big Canada Goose, nest on the coast of the Bering Sea, near the delta of the Yukon River in Alaska. They journey south, crossing part of the Pacific Ocean, then they cross the coast of the state of Washington and fly down to Tule Lake in California. They fly through passes in the mountains and settle down on the Sacramento Refuge. Vast flocks of Pintail Ducks winter here, too.

A main highway runs along the side of the Sacramento Wildlife Refuge. Sometimes this highway is almost blocked by the cars of people stopping to watch the thousands of Ducks and Geese feeding in the fields and swamps by the road.

Stilt
(About 15")

Bear River Migratory Refuge

The Bear River Migratory Refuge in Utah is one of the largest wildfowl refuges in the United States. Not only does it provide a resting place for migratory birds, but also for thousands of waterfowl that nest there in the summer.

Visitors are welcome at most refuges, and thousands of people go to this Utah refuge each year. Easily reached by a good highway, it is one of the best places for people to see birds by the millions. Long lines of White Pelicans come sailing in like transport airplanes. Black-necked Stilts wade on their long legs and tip down to feed in the shallow water. During the summer little flocks of Canada Geese Goslings sail through the water, following their stately mothers. Terns, snow-white Egrets, and Glossy Ibises dart here and there through the reeds.

Common Tern
(13-16")

Red Rock Lake Wildlife Refuge

One of the most beautiful refuges is the Red Rock Lake Wildlife Refuge in Montana. This refuge is nationally known for one species of bird which nests here. A few years ago there were only two colonies of Trumpeter Swans in the United States, and one of these was found by the Red Rock Lakes. A refuge was established in order to protect these great birds, which were nearly extinct. The birds have increased, and it is now fairly certain that the Trumpeter Swans have been saved.

Visit a Refuge

A visit to a bird refuge offers a good chance to see birds of many different varieties. And when the birds arrive in great flocks, it is an exciting time. Recently, we visited a refuge in California where there are huge flocks of Whistling Swans.

Egret
(38-41")

Snowy Egret
(About 25")

These birds have a wingspread of six to seven feet. Some of the birds floated majestically on the pond; others stood on the banks and preened themselves. Occasionally a new flock glided down from the sky. They set their great wings and extended their black, webbed feet as they skidded to a stop on the water.

Sandhill Cranes
(About 44″)

A large flock of Sandhill Cranes were feeding in a grain field, their deep, rolling calls sounding like distant trumpets. As we walked across the field toward them, those nearest us flew up, calling to each other and circling overhead. The great slate-gray birds, with a wingspread of six and one half to seven and one half feet, flew with necks extended and legs trailing. Their wings were held stiff and straight as they glided down again to the other side of the field. The birds walked sedately. Now and then one sprang into the air with wings spread in a strange kind of a dance.

Of course, there are thousands of acres of swampland that are not in the bird refuges. Here hunters may shoot Ducks and Geese during the hunting season. The number of birds they may shoot is controlled. When some species of Ducks or Geese become scarce, the season on that species is closed, and no one is allowed to shoot them.

Every hunter over sixteen years of age must get a migratory bird hunting license. The money obtained from the sale of these licenses is used to buy new land to make better resting and feeding grounds for the migratory birds.

Kuskokwim Wildlife Range

Birds must also be protected in the areas in which they nest. One of the newest refuges to be set aside is a vast nesting area. The Kuskokwim Wildlife Range covers two million acres on the deltas of the Kuskokwim and the Yukon Rivers in western Alaska. This new refuge is the largest migratory waterfowl nesting area in North America.

Rough-legged Hawk
(20-22")

11

Friends of the Farmer

"Where's the gun?" shouted the farmer's son as he dashed into the house, letting the screen door slam behind him. "There's a Hawk flying over the pasture. I think I can get a good shot at him." The boy grabbed the gun and raced away.

In a few minutes the boy was back with a big Swainson's Hawk. The farmer praised his son for being a good shot. Then, while they sat in the shade of the house, the farmer began to complain about the gophers that were digging up the pasture.

100

Swainson's Hawk
(20-22")

"I can hardly cross the field without my horse stepping in a gopher hole," he said. "And the mice are in the grain field again."

"We must do something about the rabbits," his wife called from the porch. "They've eaten all the lettuce in the garden."

The farmer did not know that the Hawk, which lay at his feet, had killed hundreds of mice, rabbits, moles, and gophers each year. He did not know that this very Hawk had been soaring over the field, looking for rodents, when the gun brought it down.

There are several different kinds of Hawks. The Swainson belongs to a group of broad-winged, soaring Hawks. It is easy for the farmer to recognize these helpful Hawks, for they usually soar over the fields with their tails spread in the shape of a fan. The broad-winged Hawks live almost entirely on gophers, ground squirrels, rabbits, mice, snakes, and insects. These birds are the farmers' friends.

Rough-legged Hawk
(20-22")

The swift-flying Hawks do not soar as do the broad-winged Hawks. The swift flyers dart out of the forest and catch small birds. The larger of such Hawks preys on Chickens. The farmer can identify these harmful Hawks by their narrow, pointed wings.

Most of these swift-flying Hawks are considered harmful, because they destroy many of the insect-eating and seed-eating birds. The smallest member of this group, however, is a friend of the farmer. This little Hawk is called a Sparrow Hawk, although it seldom catches Sparrows. Its food is crickets, grasshoppers, caterpillars, spiders, and mice.

Sparrow Hawk
(About 12")

Sparrow Hawks are found in most parts of North America. This small bird is easily recognized because it flies swiftly and often stops to hover with fluttering wings over a field. It often sits on telephone wires and posts, and, in this position, it is an easy mark. Anyone who can carry a gun can shoot a Sparrow Hawk, the law permitting. But everyone should remember that this bird is one of the farmer's best friends.

Burrowing Owl
(About 9″)

Owls

Rats, mice, and rabbits are most active at night and it is during the night hours that the Owl goes hunting. The Department of Agriculture estimates that each Owl catches about a thousand mice a year. Mice destroy grain, and, in the forests and orchards, they gnaw at the bark of the young trees, which eventually kills the trees.

Horned Owl
(About 25″)

Rabbits would do far more damage if the large Owls were not gliding over the fields on silent wings, watching for them. Scientists estimate that one Barn Owl will do away with more mice than a dozen house cats. And, of course, the Great Horned Owl will catch more rabbits than the farmer's dog.

The Sparrow-Finch family is the largest of all bird families. There are many different species of Sparrows and Finches, and every one of these eats seeds.

The field below our house was infested with thistles. Hundreds of these plants sprang up along the driveway. But just as soon as the thistle heads were ripe, a flock of Goldfinches came. They lived in the field for weeks, tearing open the thistle heads and eating the seeds.

Goldfinch
(4½-6″)

Many Sparrows do not migrate in the fall. Those that stay on the farms and around the gardens all winter are busy all day scratching away the dead leaves and hunting for the fallen seeds. Bobwhite and Quail stay all winter in most parts of the United States. They eat weed seeds as well as insects.

Bobwhite
(9½-10¾")

Scavenger Birds

Another group of birds is valuable in a very different way. These are the scavenger birds. The best known scavenger bird is the Turkey Vulture, Buzzard, as it is often called. The Buzzard soars over the country hunting for dead animals. If an animal dies in the woods or fields, the Buzzards come and eat the carcass, thus keeping the woods clean.

The Gull, another scavenger, performs a very important function around the ports and beaches. Gulls fly up and down

Turkey Vulture
(26-32″)

the beaches summer and winter, looking for some bits of food that have been cast up by the waves. These birds soon dispose of the dead creatures which would make the seashore unpleasant. Gulls eat many insects, too. Along the seacoast and lakes they feed in the fields. Flocks of Gulls follow the farmer as he plows. The birds feed on grasshoppers, which jump as the plow passes by.

Many years ago, the early settlers in Utah were saved from starvation by the Gulls. Flying insects came in great clouds. They settled on the fields of grain and corn and covered the

Laughing Gull
(About 17″)

Herring Gull
(26″)

gardens. In every way they knew, the people tried to get rid of the insects. If their crops were destroyed, there would be no food to eat.

Then came great flocks of Gulls. They settled on the fields and greedily ate the insects. They stayed until all the insects were gone, and the farmers' fields were saved. Today a tall monument stands in Salt Lake City—a grateful memorial to the Gulls that saved the early settlers from starvation.

I 2

Visitors in the Garden

Birds are creatures of the wild and are dependent on nature for all they need to maintain life. They get their food wherever they can find it. True, they will eat some of the farmer's fruit and berries, and some of his grain, too. They may pull up some young plants or nip off the tiny lettuce leaves. But usually, the birds more than make up for this by eating weed seeds and destroying harmful insects. And because the farmer and the gardener realize what good friends birds are to man, they do what they can to invite the birds to stay nearby.

There are many ways to attract birds. Different species are attracted in different ways. Birds that eat insects will also eat nuts, sunflower seeds, suet, and other foods that supply their bodies with fat.

Red-bellied Woodpecker
(About 10″)

Suet, the fat part of beef, is food for such birds as Nut-hatches, Chickadees, and Woodpeckers. You can buy a big chunk of suet at a butcher shop for only a few cents. Wrap some coarse wire, such as chicken wire, around a small piece of suet. Then drive a nail through the mass and fasten it to a tree or a stump. The birds can peck through the wire screen, but the Jays and squirrels can not carry away the whole chunk.

Suet Candle

When we prepared some suet in a different way, the birds were our constant visitors. We heated the suet in a pan until it was melted. Next, we mixed the fat with peanut butter (the chunky kind is best). Then we stirred in cracked grains and chick feed, and we poured the whole mixture into frozen juice cans. When the mixture was cold and solid, we cut the bottom out of the can. Then we fastened the can to a tree by driving a long nail through it.

Blue Jay
(About 12″)

The birds were soon working at each end of the can. Blue Jays were the first to find it. They inspected it carefully before they sampled the food. Then they ate their fill. The Chickadees, Woodpeckers, and Nuthatches were regular customers at the lunch can.

Feeding Tray

Birds that eat seeds come to the feeding tray near the window. They like chick feed, bread crumbs, and chopped nuts. All summer we save cantaloupe and watermelon seeds. We wash and dry them and store them in a jar. In winter we put these on the feeding tray. Nuthatches carry the seeds to a big oak in the yard. There they wedge and hammer the seeds into cracks in the bark. If they are hungry, they stop and pick the seeds open; if they are not, they hide the seeds and dash back to the tray for more food.

It is always fun to have a feeding tray near the window where you can watch your visitors. The tray need not be elaborate. Just a board on the window sill will do. An outside edge to keep the seeds from blowing off is a good idea. Some people put a feeding tray a little farther from the house so that the timid birds

110

Feeding Tray

will not be afraid to use it. Most birds seem to like a tray near a shrub or a tree. In that way, they can drop down onto the tray and fly quickly back to the tree if danger threatens.

We use a log in the yard as a feeding station. This has several advantages. The grain and scraps fall into the cracks in the bark and are not blown away by the wind or washed off by the rain; and the rough bark gives the birds something to cling to when they alight.

Ground birds, such as Towhees and Quail, will approach grain and seeds thrown on the ground. One farmer made a wigwam of shocks of wheat in the corner of his garden. He kept grain inside and around the wigwam. This provided a place to put feed, and it also protected the birds from wind and snow.

Birds are attracted to berries, such as juniper, barberry, holly, and thornapples. Thrushes and Cedar Waxwings will stay near the garden until all the berries are gone. A neighbor leaves some of the fruit on her persimmon tree each fall. All winter she has many bird visitors pecking at the persimmons. A farmer may attract birds by leaving brushy corners in the fields and fence rows. Here, Sparrows and Quail will find shelter and food. They will repay the farmer by cleaning out weed seeds and insects in the surrounding fields.

Martin Birdhouse

Bird Homes

There are over thirty species of birds in North America that nest in holes of trees. When dead trees are cut down and dead branches cut away, birds have a hard time finding nesting cavities. Many of these birds will nest in boxes. It is a wise farmer and gardener who puts up nesting boxes. Birds will stay in his yard, if they can find a place to nest.

Bluebirds are easily persuaded to nest in a nesting box. Nuthatches and some kinds of Swallows will accept man-made homes. House Wrens, Chickadees, Woodpeckers, and Martins are among the birds that seem to like a box built to fit. Martins are community birds and will live in a house that holds many families. A busy houseful of Martins is a joy in any yard. The Purple Martin can scoop up two thousand mosquitoes in a day. The Indians called the Martin "the bird that never rests."

112

Brown Towhee
(8½-10")

There are a few rules to remember when making a bird-house. In your public library, you can find books that tell you exactly what kinds of houses will attract the birds that live in your neighborhood. A birdhouse should be plain and inconspicuous—it should look as natural as possible. Boxes should not be too close to each other. Unlike the Martins, most birds want their homes quite widely separated.

The birdhouse must have a removable roof or side so that it can be cleaned out each winter. The box must be placed where it can not be reached by cats.

Purple Martin
(7-8½")

It is important that the opening in the birdhouse be the right size. Directions for building the house will tell the size needed for each bird. If the hole seems to be too small, remember that a bird wants space just large enough for it to squeeze through. Birds are usually not so plump as they appear, and their fluffed-out feathers make them look larger than they really are. It is always amazing that a Wren can enter so tiny a hole. The entrance to a Wren's home should be about the size of a fifty-cent piece, and the hole should be about two inches from the top of the box. Birds do not want to be seen while sitting.

No nesting material should be placed in the box. Leave that to the birds. Material may be placed in the garden where the birds can find it. Bits of wool, yarn, string, and wisps of cotton will be carried away by birds and used for building their nests.

Wren Birdhouse

114

Protecting Natural Resources

Birds and their ways are wonderfully interesting, but the benefits they bring us are far more important than their color or song. They are an irreplaceable natural resource, and the extinction of any species might upset the balance of nature.

When birds are driven away, uncontrolled increase of insect pests often follows. This in turn requires the use of chemical insecticides to control the insect population. Unfortunately, chemicals are neither as attractive, nor as selective as birds. Besides killing off birds and harmless insects, chemical sprays often pollute our streams and rivers thereby affecting even fish.

Although the Passenger Pigeon is gone forever, it may not yet be too late to save the Whooping Crane, the Trumpeter Swan and the Condor, among others. To this end, the Federal Government together with the individual states are setting aside areas for wildlife refuges. As individuals, we too can help by providing safe resting places in our own yards where birds can find water and food.

Let us hope that our meadowlands and forests will continue to resound with the songs of birds, forever delighting mankind.

Loons

Chart of Nor
Indicating Re

Of the 27 orders of living birds of the world, 20 orders are represented in North America. They are given here in the systematic classification followed by ornithologists. This classification is based largely on various internal features of the birds—skeleton structure, etc.—and on some external features, such as the bill and the number of primary feathers. When following this grouping, a list of North American birds always starts with Loons and ends with Grosbeaks, Finches, Sparrows, and Buntings.

The exact num
ornithological sys
on every detail
gists agree that t
throughout the w
the world, not j
The numbers giv
nized by ornithol

ORDER	FAMILY	SPECIES IN FAMILY	
		World[1]	North Ame
Gaviiformes Loons	Loons	4	4
Podicipediformes Grebes	Grebes	20	6
Procellariiformes Shearwaters and Related Families	Albatrosses	13	5 (+ 1 Greenland
	Fulmars, Shearwaters	53	17 (+ 2 Baja Calif + 1 Bermuda)
	Storm Petrels	20	9 (+ 2 Baja Calif

[1] World figures from Ernst Mayr and Dean Amadon, "A Classification of Recent Birds," in *American Museum Novitates* (New York, April 2, 1951), No. 1496.

[2] North American figures based on American Ornithologists' Union, *Check-list of North American Birds* (5th edition, 1957). The area covered by the *Check-list* is defined by the A. O. U. as "North America north of

Mexico, with inclusion
this summary list, spe
California, but not on n
reader should also remember that oceanic
waters, Storm Petrels, Tropicbirds, and Frigatebirds are usually seen at
sea, for they do not ordinarily come to North American shores.

ORDER	FAMILY	SPECIES IN FAMILY		REPRESENTATIVE SPECIES
		World	North America	
Pelecaniformes Tropicbirds, Pelicans, Frigatebirds, and Related Families	Tropicbirds Pelicans Boobies, Gannets Cormorants Darters Frigatebirds	3 6 9 30 1 5	3 2 5 6 1 1	White-tailed Tropicbird White Pelican Gannet Double-crested Cormorant Anhinga Magnificent Frigatebird
Ciconiiformes Herons, Storks, Ibises, Flamingos, and Related Families	Herons, Bitterns Storks, Wood Ibises Ibises, Spoonbills Flamingos	59 17 28 6	14 (+ 1 Greenland) 1 5 (+ 1 Greenland) 1	Great Blue Heron Wood Ibis[3] Glossy Ibis American Flamingo
Anseriformes Waterfowl	Swans, Geese, Ducks	145	60 (+ 1 Bermuda; + 1 Greenland; 1 extinct, Labrador Duck)	Whistling Swan, Canada Goose, Mallard Duck
Falconiformes Diurnal (active during the day) Birds of Prey	American Vultures[4] Hawks, Old World Vultures, Harriers Ospreys Caracaras, Falcons	6 205 1 58	3 (+ 1 formerly in Florida) 25 1 8 (+ 1 Baja California, now extinct)	Turkey Vulture, California Condor Red-tailed Hawk, Golden Eagle Osprey Sparrow Hawk

Great Blue Heron

Rough-legged Hawk

[3] The Wood Ibis has been called Wood Stork also, a name which helps one to remember that it is actually a member of the Stork-Wood Ibis family and not of the Ibis-Spoonbill family.
[4] The Vultures mentioned in this book are members of this family.

ORDER	FAMILY	SPECIES IN FAMILY World	SPECIES IN FAMILY North America	REPRESENTATIVE SPECIES
Galliformes Gallinaceous (Chickenlike) Birds	Curassows, Guans, Chachalacas	38	1	Chachalaca
	Grouse, Ptarmigan	18	10	Ruffed Grouse
	Quails, Pheasants, Peacocks	165	9	Bobwhite
	Turkeys	2	1	Turkey
Gruiformes Marsh Birds	Cranes	14	2	Sandhill Crane, Whooping Crane
	Limpkins	1	1	Limpkin
	Rails, Gallinules, Coots	132	10 (+ 2 Greenland)	Common Gallinule
Charadriiformes Shorebirds, Gulls, Auks, and Related Families	Jaçanas	7	1	Jaçana
	Oystercatchers	6	2 (+ 1 Greenland)	American Oystercatcher
	Plovers, Turnstones, Surfbirds	63	15 (+ 1 Greenland)	American Golden Plover, Ruddy Turnstone
	Woodcock, Snipe, Sandpipers	77	44 (+ 1 Greenland)	Common Snipe, Spotted Sandpiper
	Avocets, Stilts	7	2	Black-necked Stilt
	Phalaropes	3	3	Northern Phalarope
	Jaegers, Skuas	4	4	Pomarine Jaeger
	Gulls, Terns	82	40	Herring Gull, Arctic Tern
	Skimmers	3	1	Black Skimmer
	Auks, Murres, Puffins	22	20 (+1 extinct—Great Auk)	Common Puffin
Columbiformes Pigeonlike Birds	Pigeons, Doves	289	15 (+ 1 extinct— Passenger Pigeon)	Mourning Dove
Psittaciformes Parrotlike Birds	Lories, Parrots, Macaws	316	1 (+ 1 extinct— Carolina Parakeet)	Thick-billed Parrot

Ruffed Grouse

Spotted Sandpiper

ORDER	FAMILY	SPECIES IN FAMILY		REPRESENTATIVE SPECIES
		World	North America	
Cuculiformes Cuckoos and Related Family	Cuckoos, Roadrunners, Anis	128	7	Yellow-billed Cuckoo, Roadrunner
Strigiformes Owls (nocturnal, or active at night, birds of prey)	Barn Owls	11	1	Barn Owl
	Typical Owls	123	17	Screech Owl, Great Horned Owl
Caprimulgiformes Goatsuckers and Related Families	Goatsuckers	67	6	Whip-poor-will, Common Nighthawk
Apodiformes Swifts, Hummingbirds	Swifts	79	6	Chimney Swift
	Hummingbirds	319	17 (+ 1 Baja California)	Ruby-throated Hummingbird
Trogoniformes Trogons	Trogons	35	1	Coppery-tailed Trogon
Coraciiformes Kingfishers and Related Families	Kingfishers	87	3	Belted Kingfisher
Piciformes Woodpeckers and Related Families	Woodpeckers, Wrynecks	210	23	Yellow-shafted Flicker, Hairy Woodpecker
Passeriformes Perching Birds	Cotingas	90	1	Rose-throated Becard
	Tyrant Flycatchers[5]	365	32	Kingbird (Eastern, Western)
	Larks	75	2	Horned Lark
	Swallows	75	11 (+ 1 Greenland)	Barn Swallow
	Jays, Magpies, Crows	100	16 (+ 2 Greenland)	Blue Jay, Common Crow
	Titmice, Verdins, Bushtits	64	14	Black-capped Chickadee, Tufted Titmouse
	Nuthatches	29	4	White-breasted Nuthatch
	Creepers[6]	6	1	Brown Creeper

Horned Owl

Barn Swallow

Nuthatch

ORDER	FAMILY	SPECIES IN FAMILY		REPRESENTATIVE SPECIES
		World	North America	
Passeriformes (cont'd)	Wrentits (with Babblers)	282	1	Wrentit
	Dippers	5	1	Dipper
	Wrens	63	10	House Wren
	Mockingbirds, Thrashers	30	10 (+ 1 Baja California)	Mockingbird, Brown Thrasher
	Thrushes, Solitaires, Bluebirds	304	14 (+ 3 Greenland; + 1 Baja California)	Robin, Wood Thrush, Eastern Bluebird
	Old World Warblers, Gnatcatchers, Kinglets	313	6 (+1 Greenland)	Blue-gray Gnatcatcher, Ruby-crowned Kinglet
	Accentors	12	1	Mountain Accentor (An Asian bird which has been seen in Alaska)
	Wagtails, Pipits	48	6 (+ 1 Greenland)	Water Pipit
	Waxwings	3	2	Cedar Waxwing
	Silky Flycatchers	4	1	Phainopepla
	Shrikes	67	2	Loggerhead Shrike
	Starlings	103	2	Starling
	Vireos	41	12	Red-eyed Vireo
	Honeycreepers	36	1	Bahama Honeycreeper
	Wood Warblers[7]	109	54 (+ 3 Baja California)	Myrtle Warbler, American Redstart
	Weaver Finches	263	2	House Sparrow ("English" Sparrow)
	Meadowlarks, Blackbirds, Orioles	88	22	Meadowlark (Eastern, Western), Baltimore Oriole, Common Grackle
	Tanagers	196	4	Scarlet Tanager
	Grosbeaks, Finches, Sparrows, Buntings[8]	425	85 (+ 4 Baja California)	Cardinal, American Goldfinch, Song Sparrow, Snow Bunting

Sparrow

Meadowlark

Thrush

Cedar Waxwing

[5] The Flycatchers mentioned in this book are members of the Tyrant Flycatcher family.
[6] The Creepers mentioned in this book are members of this family.
[7] The Warblers mentioned in this book are members of the Wood Warbler family.
[8] The Finches mentioned in this book are members of this family.

14
List of National Wildlife Refuges

ALABAMA
Choctaw, Choctaw Co.; Wheeler, Morgan, Limestone & Madison Cos.

ALASKA
Aleutian Islands, 3d div.; Bering Sea, 2nd div.; Bogoslof, 3d div.; Chamisso, 2nd div.; Clarence Rhode National Wildlife Range, 4th & 2nd divs.; Forrester Island, 1st div.; Hazen Bay, 4th div.; Hazy Islands, 1st div.; Izembek National Wildlife Range, 3d div.; Kenai National Moose Range, 3d div.; Kodiak, 3d div.; Nunivak, 2nd div.; Pribilof Reservation, 3d div.; St. Lazaria, 1st div.; Semidi, 3d div.; Simenof, 3d div.; Tuxedni, 3d div.

ARIZONA
Cabeza Prieta Game Range, Yuma, Pima Co.; Havasu Lake (*see also* California), Mohave, Yuma Co.; Imperial (*see also* California), Yuma Co.; Kofa Game Range, Yuma Co.

ARKANSAS
Big Lake, Mississippi Co.; Holla Bend, Pope Co.; Wapanocca, Crittenden Co.; White River, Arkansas, Desha, Monroe & Phillips Cos.

CALIFORNIA
Clear Lake, Modoc Co.; Colusa, Colusa Co.; Delevan, Colusa Co.; Farallon, Marin Co.; Havasu Lake (*see also* Arizona), San Bernardino Co.; Imperial (*see also* Arizona), Imperial Co.; Kern, Kern Co.; Lower Klamath (*see also* Oregon), Siskiyou Co.; Merced, Merced Co.; Modoc, Modoc Co.; Pixley, Tulare Co.; Sacramento, Glenn & Colusa Cos.; Salton Sea, Imperial Co.; Sutter, Sutter Co.; Tule Lake, Modoc & Siskiyou Cos.

COLORADO
Alamosa, Alamosa Co.; Monte Vista, Alamosa & Rio Grande Cos.

DELAWARE
Bombay Hook, Kent Co.; Killcohook (*see also* New Jersey), New Castle Co.; Primehook, Sussex Co.

FLORIDA
Anclote, Pasco & Pinellas Cos.; Brevard, Brevard Co.; Cedar Keys, Levy Co.; Chassahowitzka, Hernando Co.; Great White Heron Monroe Co.; Island Bay, Charlotte Co.; Key West, Monroe Co.; Loxahatchee, Palm Beach & Broward Cos.; National Key Deer, Monroe Co.; Passage Key, Manatee Co.; Pelican Island, Indian River Co.; Pinellas, Pinellas Co.; St. Marks, Jefferson, Taylor & Wakulla Cos.; Sanibel, Lee Co.

GEORGIA
Blackbeard Island, McIntosh Co.; Harris Neck, McIntosh Co.; Okefenokee, Charlton, Clinch & Ware Cos.; Piedmont, Jones & Jasper Cos.; Savannah (*see also* South Carolina), Chatham Co.; Tybee, Chatham Co.; Wolfe Island, McIntosh Co.

HAWAII
Hawaiian Islands, Kauai Co.

IDAHO
Camas, Jefferson Co.; Deer Flat, Canyon Co.; Minidoka, Cassia, Blaine, Power & Minidoka Cos.

ILLINOIS
Chautauqua, Mason Co.; Crab Orchard, Williamson, Jackson & Union Cos.; Mark Twain (*see also* Iowa & Missouri), Adams, Calhoun, Jersey & Mercer Cos.; Upper Mississippi River Wild Life and Fish Refuge (*see also* Iowa, Minnesota & Wisconsin), Carroll, Jo Daviess, Rock Island & Whiteside Cos.

IOWA
De Soto (*see also* Nebraska), Harrison & Pottawattamie Cos.; Mark Twain (*see also* Illinois & Missouri), Des Moines, Louisa & Muscatine Cos.; Union Slough, Kossuth Co.; Upper Mississippi River Wild Life & Fish Refuge (*see also* Illinois, Minnesota & Wisconsin), all counties along the river, from Scott County north.

KANSAS
Kirwin, Phillips Co.; Quivira, Stafford & Rice Cos.

KENTUCKY
Kentucky Woodlands, Trigg & Lyon Cos.; Reelfoot (*see also* Tennessee), Fulton Co.

LOUISIANA
Breton, Plaquemines Co.; Catahoula, LaSalle Co.; Delta, Plaquemines Co.; East Timbalier Island, Terrebonne Co.; Lacassine, Cameron Co.; Sabine, Cameron Co.; Shell Keys, Iberia Co.

MAINE
Moosehorn, Washington Co.

MARYLAND
Blackwater, Dorchester Co.; Chincoteague (*see also* Virginia), Somerset Co.; Eastern Neck, Kent Co.; Martin, Somerset Co.; Susquehanna, Hartford & Cecil Cos.

MASSACHUSETTS
Great Meadows, Essex Co.; Monomoy, Barnstable Co.; Parker River, Essex Co.

MICHIGAN
Huron, Marquette Co.; Lake St. Clair, St. Clair & Macomb Cos.; Michigan Islands, Alpena & Charlevoix Cos.; Seney, Schoolcraft Co.; Shiawassee, Saginaw Co.; Wyandotte, Wayne Co.

MINNESOTA
Agassiz (formerly Mud Lake), Marshall Co.; Mille Lacs, Mille Lacs Co.; Rice Lake, Aitkin Co.; Tamarac, Becker Co.; Upper Mississippi River Wild Life & Fish Refuge (*see also* Illinois, Iowa & Wisconsin), Houston, Winona, Wabasha & Goodhue Cos.

MISSISSIPPI
Davis Island, Warren Co.; Horn Island, Jackson Co.; Noxubee, Winston, Noxubee & Oktibbeha Cos.; Petit Bois, Jackson Co.; Yazoo, Washington Co.

MISSOURI
Mark Twain (*see also* Iowa & Illinois), St. Charles Co.; Mingo, Wayne & Stoddard Cos.; Squaw Creek, Holt Co.; Swan Lake, Charlton Co.

MONTANA
Benton Lake, Cascade & Chouteau Cos.; Black Coulee, Blaine Co.; Bowdoin, Phillips Co.; Charles M. Russell National Wildlife Range, Valley, Garfield, Petroleum, Fergus, Phillips & McCone Cos.; Creedman Coulee, Hill Co.; Hailstone, Stillwater Co.; Halfbreed Lake, Stillwater Co.; Hewitt Lake, Phillips Co.; Lake Mason, Musselshell Co.; Lake Thibadeau, Hill Co.; Lamesteer, Wibaux Co.; Medicine Lake, Roosevelt & Sheridan Cos.; National Bison Range, Sanders & Lake Cos.; Nine-Pipe, Lake Co.; Pablo, Lake Co.; Pishkun, Teton Co.; Red Rock Lakes, Beaverhead Co.; War Horse, Petroleum Co.; Willow Creek, Lewis & Clark Cos.

NEBRASKA
Crescent Lake, Garden Co.; De Soto (*see also* Iowa), Washington Co.; Fort Niobrara, Cherry Co.; North Platte, Scottsbluff & Sioux Cos.; Valentine, Cherry Co.

NEVADA
Anaho Island, Washoe Co.; Charles Sheldon Antelope Range (*see also* Oregon), Washoe & Humboldt Cos.; Desert Game Range, Clark & Lincoln Cos.; Fallon, Churchill Co.; Ruby Lake, Elko & White Pine Cos.; Stillwater, Churchill Co.

NEW JERSEY
Brigantine, Atlantic Co.; Great Swamp, Morris Co.; Killcohook (*see also* Delaware), Salem Co.; Troy Meadows, Morris Co.

NEW MEXICO
Bitter Lake, Chaves Co.; Bosque del Apache, Socorro Co.; Burford Lake, Rio Arriba Co.; San Andres, Dona Ana Co.

NEW YORK
Elizabeth Alexandra Morton, Suffolk Co.; Montezuma, Seneca Co.; Oak Orchard, Genesee & Orleans Cos.; Wertheim, Suffolk Co.

NORTH CAROLINA
Mackay Island (*see also* Virginia), Currituck Co.; Mattamuskeet, Hyde Co.; Pea Island, Dare Co.; Swanquarter, Hyde Co.

NORTH DAKOTA
Appert Lake, Emmons Co.; Ardoch, Walsh Co.; Arrowwood, Stutsman & Foster Cos.; Bone Hill, LaMoure Co.; Brumba, Towner Co.; Buffalo Lake, Pierce Co.; Camp Lake, McLean Co.; Canfield Lake, Burleigh Co.; Chase Lake, Stutsman Co.; Cottonwood Lake, McHenry Co.; Dakota Lake, Dickey Co.; Des Lacs, Burke & Ward Cos.; Flickertail, Emmons Co.; Florence Lake, Burleigh Co.; Half-Way Lake, Stutsman Co.; Hiddenwood, McLean & Ward Cos.; Hobart Lake, Barnes Co.; Hutchinson Lake, Kidder Co.; Johnson Lake, Nelson & Eddy Cos.; Kellys Slough, Grand Forks Co.; Lac Aux Mortes, Ramsey Co.; Lake Elsie, Richland Co.; Lake George, Kidder Co.; Lake Ilo, Dunn Co.; Lake Nettie, McLean Co.; Lake Zahl, Williams Co.; Lambs

Lake, Nelson Co.; Little Goose, Grand Forks Co.; Long Lake, Burleigh & Kidder Cos.; Lords Lake, Bottineau & Rolette Cos.; Lost Lake, McLean Co.; Lostwood, Burke & Mountrail Cos.; Lower Souris, Bottineau & McHenry Cos.; Maple River, Dickey Co.; McLean, McLean Co.; Pleasant Lake, Benson Co.; Pretty Rock, Grant Co.; Rabb Lake, Rolette Co.; Rock Lake, Towner Co.; Rose Lake, Nelson Co.; School Section Lake, Rolette Co.; Shell Lake, Mountrail Co.; Sheyenne Lake, Sheridan Co.; Sibley Lake, Griggs Co.; Silver Lake, Benson & Ramsey Cos.; Slade, Kidder Co.; Snake Creek, McLean Co.; Snyder Lake, Towner Co.; Springwater, Emmons Co.; Stewart Lake, Slope Co.; Stoney Slough, Barnes Co.; Storm Lake, Sargent Co.; Stump Lake, Nelson Co.; Sullys Hill National Game Preserve, Benson Co.; Sunburst Lake, Emmons Co.; Tewaukon, Sargent Co.; Tomahawk, Barnes Co.; Upper Souris, Renville & Ward Cos.; White Lake, Slope Co.; Wild Rice Lake, Sargent Co.; Willow Lake, Rolette Co.; Wintering River, McHenry Co.; Wood Lake, Benson Co.

OHIO
Ottawa, Lucas & Ottawa Cos.; West Sister Island, Lucas Co.

OKLAHOMA
Salt Plains, Alfalfa Co.; Tishomingo, Johnston & Marshall Cos.; Washita, Custer Co.; Wichita Mountains Wildlife Refuge, Comanche Co.

OREGON
Cape Meares, Tillamook Co.; Charles Sheldon Antelope Range (see also Nevada), Lake Co.; Cold Springs, Umatilla Co.; Hart Mountain National Antelope Refuge, Lake Co.; Klamath Forest, Klamath Co.; Lower Klamath (see also California), Klamath Co.; Malheur, Harney Co.; McKay Creek, Umatilla Co.; Oregon Islands, Curry Co.; Three Arch Rocks, Tillamook Co.; Upper Klamath, Klamath Co.

PENNSYLVANIA
Erie, Crawford Co.

SOUTH CAROLINA
Cape Romain, Charleston Co.; Carolina Sandhills, Chesterfield Co.; Santee, Clarendon & Berkeley Cos.; Savannah (see also Georgia), Jasper Co.

SOUTH DAKOTA
Bear Butte, Meade Co.; Belle Fourche, Butte Co.; Lacreek, Bennett Co.; Lake Andes, Charles Mix Co.; Sand Lake, Brown Co.; Waubay, Day Co.

TENNESSEE
Cross Creeks, Stewart Co.; Lake Isom, Lake & Obion Cos.; Reelfoot (see also Kentucky), Lake & Obion Cos.; Tennessee, Henry, Benton, Humphreys & Decatur Cos.

TEXAS
Aransas, Aransas, Refugio & Calhoun Cos.; Anahuac, Chambers Co.; Buffalo Lakes, Randall Co.; Hagerman, Grayson Co.; Laguna Atascosa, Cameron Co.; Muleshoe, Bailey Co.; Santa Ana, Hidalgo Co.

UTAH
Bear River Migratory Bird Refuge, Box Elder Co.; Fish Springs, Juab Co.; Locomotive Springs, Box Elder Co.; Ouray, Uintah Co.

VERMONT
Missisquoi, Franklin Co.

VIRGINIA
Back Bay, Princess Anne Co.; Chincoteague (see also Maryland), Accomack Co.; Mackay Island (see also North Carolina), Princess Anne Co.; Presquile, Chesterfield Co.

WASHINGTON
Columbia, Adams & Grant Cos.; Copalis, Grays Harbor Co.; Dungeness, Clallam Co.; Flattery Rocks, Clallam Co.; Jones Island, San Juan Co.; Little Pend Oreille, Stevens Co.; Matia Island, San Juan Co.; McNary, Walla Walla Co.; Quillayute Needles, Clallam & Jefferson Cos.; San Juan, San Juan Co.; Smith Island, Island Co.; Toppenish, Yakima Co.; Turnbull, Spokane Co.; Willapa, Pacific Co.

WISCONSIN
Gravel Island, Door Co.; Green Bay, Door Co.; Horicon, Dodge & Fond du Lac Cos.; Necedah, Juneau & Wood Cos.; Trempealeau, Trempealeau Co.; Upper Mississippi River Wild Life & Fish Refuge (see also Illinois, Iowa, Minnesota), Crawford, Buffalo, Vernon, Trempealeau, Grant & LaCrosse Cos.

WYOMING
Bamforth, Albany Co.; Hutton Lake, Albany Co.; National Elk Refuge, Teton Co.; Pathfinder, Natrona & Carbon Cos.

123

¹5
For Further Reading

FIELD GUIDES

AUDUBON LAND BIRD GUIDE (East and Central North America) by Richard H. Pough *(Doubleday & Co., Garden City, New York, 1949)*

AUDUBON WATER BIRD GUIDE by Richard H. Pough *(Doubleday & Co., Garden City, New York, 1951)*

AUDUBON WESTERN BIRD GUIDE by Richard H. Pough *(Doubleday & Co., Garden City, New York, 1957)*
  Contain information on habits of birds.

A FIELD GUIDE TO THE BIRDS by Roger Tory Peterson *(Houghton Mifflin Co., Boston, 2nd ed., 1947)*

A FIELD GUIDE TO WESTERN BIRDS by Roger Tory Peterson *(Houghton Mifflin Co., Boston, 2nd ed., 1961)*
  Standard guides for bird identification.

A GUIDE TO BIRD FINDING (East of the Mississippi) by Olin S. Pettingill, Jr. *(Oxford University Press, New York, 1951)*

A GUIDE TO BIRD FINDING (West of the Mississippi) by Olin S. Pettingill, Jr. *(Oxford University Press, New York, 1953)*
  Best birding areas, arranged by states.

NAMING THE BIRDS AT A GLANCE by Lou Blachly and Randolph Jenks *(Alfred A. Knopf, New York, 1963)*
  Beginner's guide to identification of birds by color patterns.

REFERENCE BOOKS

THE A.O.U. CHECK-LIST OF NORTH AMERICAN BIRDS by Committee of the American Ornithologists' Union *(5th ed., 1957)*
>A 691-page book listing North American birds by scientific and common names and giving range of each bird.

BIRDS OF THE NEW YORK AREA by John Bull *(Harper & Row, New York, 1964)*
>Includes over 400 species, with data on distribution trends, ecology, nesting, and migration.

GENERAL BOOKS

AMERICAN BIRDS AND WILDFLOWERS by Herbert S. Zim, *(Simon & Schuster, Inc., New York, 1950)*

AUDUBON WILDLIFE: With Selections from the Writings of John James Audubon; ed. by Edwin Way Teale *(Viking Press, New York, 1964)*

THE BIRDS by Roger Tory Peterson *(Time-Life Books, New York, 1962)*

BIRDS AND THEIR NESTS by Olive L. Earle *(William Morrow & Co., New York, 1952)*

BIRDS OVER AMERICA by Roger Tory Peterson *(Dodd, Mead & Company, New York, 2nd ed. 1964)*

THE BIRD WATCHER'S ANTHOLOGY by Roger Tory Peterson *(Harcourt, Brace & Co., New York, 1957)*

THE FIRST BOOK OF BIRDS by Margaret Williamson *(Franklin Watts, Inc., New York, 1951)*

A GUIDE TO BIRD WATCHING by Joseph J. Hickey *(Garden City Books, New York, 1953)*

THE REAL BOOK ABOUT AMAZING BIRDS by Eve Merriam *(Garden City Books, New York, 1955)*

SONG AND GARDEN BIRDS OF NORTH AMERICA by Alexander Wetmore, et al *(National Geographic Society, Washington, D.C., 1964)*

SONGBIRDS IN YOUR GARDEN by John K. Terres *(Thomas Y. Crowell Co., New York, 1953)*

16
Index

Figures in *Italics* indicate illustrations.
Boldface figures indicate Chart.
C indicates Color Section.

126